Leadership & Man

This Book Includes: Inspiring Leadership & Leadership 2.0. Mastering Leadership, Business Management & Building High Performance Teams

Peter Allen

Premium Content

Subscribe to our receive premium content on productive meetings, business success, marketing mastery, sales conversion, team management and much more

https://www.subscribepage.com/premiumcontent

Access

Inspiring Leadership

A Guide to Mastering Leadership, Business Management, Organization, Development and Building High Performance Teams

Table of Contents

Introduction

Thank you for buying this book. I hope you find it informative and useful.

The world is changing rapidly, and the competition is rising day by day. The corporate world has become one of the most challenging and essential employment fields today. The relationship between employees and the employer are being studied in detail by many. One of the most important questions related to this world is leadership and leadership skills.

Being a good leader and possessing good leadership skills is essential. There are many different styles of leadership, and a lot of people are often confused about these styles. Many people believe their leadership style is the best, but with a lot of research, it has been proven that no one leadership style is the best. Each leadership style has its use. Thus, there exists no one right way to lead in all circumstances. So, how do you traverse this complex world of leadership and management? This book will serve as a guide for you to master leadership, organization, and business management. It will also teach you how to build and develop high-performance teams and how to manage them.

There is a myth that leadership needs to be innate, and you cannot learn leadership skills. This is absolutely false. You can learn leadership skills, and also improve and develop your overall personality and attitude. You can learn to be a great leader by focusing on improving particular leadership skills. True leadership is a lifelong journey that requires constant learning and this book will help you on this journey by providing you various tips, tricks, and methods that will help you become a great and successful leader. Peter Allen, a well-renowned business leader, believes that leadership is a skill that can be acquired. While having innate talents can help you to become a good leader, they cannot make you a successful leader if you do not combine them with dedication, spirit, perseverance, and the thirst to learn. Many great leaders have admitted that they did not have any innate talent for leadership, but they still became successful because they persevered.

The corporate world is changing rapidly, and the things that were norms just a couple of years ago are now considered to be taboo. While the strength and passion of a leader are still considered to be assets, his or her lack of emotions is looked down upon. Now if the leader is not in touch with his or her emotions or does not care for his or her employees, then his or her chances of becoming successful become almost negligible. It is necessary to create a positive workplace culture and a positive personality and stick to it. You cannot be successful if you are not optimistic and positive. If you think that you are not earning success, then you should change the way you do business and change the way you lead your life as well. Changes often seem daunting but don't worry. This book contains various methods that will show you how changes are necessary and how they can be made without any risk. These changes are easy to adapt and can be incorporated into your corporate world with ease. You should also try to incorporate these changes into your personal world, as it will allow you to create a sustainable business. Having a sustainable business in the current world is necessary because it keeps on changing almost every day. Try to motivate your employees and create empowerment and engagement. Empowered employees will make your group strong and functional. You can empower employees by being an effective and inspirational leader. For instance, great leaders like Napoleon, Winston Churchill, Steve Jobs, Bill Gates, Joan of Arc, Angela Merkel etc. are or were considered to be successful leaders because they inspired their people. They are considered to be great leaders because they were able to guide their people through times of crisis. They supported creativity and innovation and used multiple methods to conquer their goals. At times, they changed their leadership styles so that they could incorporate other people into their groups. Thus, these leaders became great leaders because they were flexible, bold, and passionate.

This book will help you become a passionate, dedicated, inspiring, and successful leader as well. It will help you to develop your greatest potential as a leader. It will inspire action in you and will help you to inspire your team members as well. Remember, bad leadership has brought down not only groups and companies but even empires in the past. Bad leadership can ruin your fortune and can throw you out of the limelight. It is thus crucial to change your leadership style immediately! So, go on and read this book and change your life around!

Start now!

Chapter One: Dispelling Myths

Leadership is one of the most significant roles that a person can take on in their life. It is significant not only because of the perks and honor but also because of the duties and traits associated with it. Leadership is not an easy task. It is a prolonged process that takes time to develop. It can be confusing and frustrating at times. This is why a lot of myths are prevalent about leadership. These myths make leadership out to be a highly difficult and complex role. They also create an image that makes leadership seem to be a talent that only a few can possess. In this chapter, let us have a look at some of the most significant myths associated with leadership.

The Myth of Innate Leadership

The formation of fact/truth is a complex philosophical argument. Often when a statement is repeated enough times, people begin to accept it as a truth. Some of such statements include: "Elephants have really strong memories.", "Women are emotional and difficult to understand.", and the most common one being "Leaders cannot be made, they can only be born."

All of the above notions have been debunked except for the last one. The prevalence of the myth that 'Leaders are born and not made' is confusing. It is perhaps still prevalent due to gate-keeping practices. This stubborn notion is a myth that has hindered the growth of not only many individuals but also a lot of corporations. It is a prejudice that has led to a lot of problems. It stops the development of others as well as ourselves in attaining the title of great leader.

First things first, not everyone wants to be a leader. Not everyone believes leadership is an attractive position. They do not want to spend time becoming a leader. This is a valid opinion. But this does not mean that these people are not capable of leadership. Everyone can be a leader if they want to be. This is because leadership is a set of practices that can be learned through observation. Many people do not think that they can be a leader just because they have been fed this information since the beginning.

A lot of studies have been done on this topic of nature vs nurture. According to almost all researchers, there are certain 'natural' factors that can make us great leaders. For instance, the degree of intelligence, our social skills, innate empathy etc. According to some researchers, around 30% of our innate talents can help us turn into a great leader. The remaining 70% can only be learned through practice and observation. Your 30% innate talent will be useless if you do not learn how to use it and combine it with the remaining 70% of observation. Thus, nature and nurture are both equally responsible for creating a great leader.

People who genuinely believe that leaders are born and not made will always have a different point of view toward leadership. They will believe it to be a formal and autonomous position. People who believe that leaders are born will also believe in their authoritarian power. They will believe that a leader can only be successful if they follow the protocols of hierarchy. For them, formality makes the best and most successful leaders. Such people think that only rule-abiding leaders can be successful. In contrast to this, people who believe that leaders are not born and are rather made will always look at leadership as a collective and collaborative endeavor. For them, teams make leaders and not vice versa.

The beliefs related to 'made' and 'born' leaders also affect our selection of leaders. Teams who believe that leadership is an innate quality will always choose a person who seems to be a leader ignoring the later development a person may undergo. Expecting a person to be a great leader just because of a few innate qualities can prove harmful to the mental health of the individual and the strength of the company.

Thus, if you want to become a great leader or want to choose a great leader, then you should try to seek a balance between 'nature and nurture.'

Developing a leader is not a scientific activity; rather, it is an artistic endeavor. Like an artist, a leader should possess some sort of conceptual knowledge and innate skills. An artist can benefit a lot if he or she possesses these skills, but their art cannot progress if they do not practice it regularly. Similarly, a leader cannot become successful and grow in his or her field until he or she practices and learns from observation.

If you want to become a great leader, just focus on your surroundings and your work. Try to maintain cordial relationships with everyone. You need to learn how to observe things and how to utilize them for your own benefits. This will allow you to become a successful leader soon.

In the end, you should remember that anyone could excel at anything if they are dedicated and passionate about it. Leadership is a skill and not a genetic trait. Here is a quote to keep you inspired.

"Leaders aren't born; they are made. And they are made just like anything else, through hard work. And that's the price we'll have to pay to achieve that goal or any goal." - Vince Lombardi

Leadership is possessing powers over others

One of the biggest myths associated with leadership is that leaders are omnipotent. You cannot be a leader unless you possess power others and dominate them. This is an unfortunate myth that perpetuates the stereotype of a selfish and angry boss. This creates a negative atmosphere in the workplace, which leads to a lot of problems later. A company cannot progress unless a positive workplace atmosphere is maintained for which, the team and the team leader both need to understand their positions.

There have been a lot of selfish leaders who have only focused on their personal gains and development often while sacrificing others. It is said that power can corrupt even the best of people. This has been proven by many examples in the past; however, it is still a myth. Power does not corrupt people, rather the notions associated with power and the theories perpetuated about it, and corrupt people.

Leaders try to control their employees to get what they want. They like to dominate others to do their bidding. This kind of negative and narcissistic behaviour can ruin a company. Not all leaders act like this now. The notions and concept of leadership have undergone significant changes in the past few decades.

The pace of life and the level of competition has drastically changed in the modern world. Businesses, employees, and employers all have become action-oriented. People often believe that sometimes you need to sacrifice others for the greater good. Often the employees and team members become the 'sacrificial goats.'

Leaders who are disconnected from themselves and their team members continue to act in ways that can hider interpersonal connections. Leadership is not a struggle for power; rather, it is a nourishing and balancing endeavor. A leader not only needs to nourish his or her team members but also maintain a balance between their work and attitude.

A leader cannot be power-hungry, as it will destroy the harmony in the team. Dominance and respect are like yin and yang; you need both to control and guide people. Maintaining a balance between these two is crucial, or you will become an unpopular leader soon.

Static Leadership

Another aspect related to power-hungriness and leadership is the belief that leadership is static. Many people (including many leaders) believe that once a person becomes a leader, they continue to be a leader throughout their life. In reality, leadership is rarely this static; rather, it is dynamic, effective, and alive. It changes frequently.

Thus, everyone is a leader in away. You do not need to be in the front to lead people; you can also inspire and guide people from the back or even outside the team. You will find out more about this in the subsequent section.

Leaders are positively influential

People believe that leaders are heroic, smart, and intelligent. They believe that all leaders possess excellent problem-solving capabilities and that they can tackle even the most complex of problems and come up with solutions almost instantaneously. They believe that leaders can change the world for good on their own. This goes against all the collaborative and inclusive practices that leaders are supposed to undertake. This kind of reading of leaders is not only shallow but is quite one-dimensional as well.

It is true that leaders can be influential, but not all leaders are good. Many times, the solutions put forward by leaders are ineffective because they do not undergo rigorous and committed debate with the situation. Three things are essential if you want to become a great leader: Critical thinking, curiosity, and inclusiveness.

Leaders who can be a positive influence on others include leaders who understand their strengths and weaknesses. People who understand their own limitations know what their problems are, and they often work in the direction to solve or get rid of them. Leadership is a team sport. You cannot play it without collaborative efforts. Leaders understand that they need a diverse team to influence people. They understand that if they truly want to innovate, they will need to put a lot of efforts.

Everyone knows that great leaders are often great speakers. But not many people know that to be a great leader, you also need to be a great listener as well. Great leaders understand that their role in the team is to understand and inspire and not to answer others. They know that they are supposed to hire excellent people and get regular inputs from them. They understand their mistakes and allow others to correct them.

Leaders can inspire and empower others to become great leaders. Their ultimate goal is their best version. They should create a team that can work just as well, even if they are not present.

Tom Peters once said: "Leaders don't create more followers; they create more leaders." This quote shows how leaders can help the innate talents of people develop.

A negative aspect associated with leadership is that leaders do not like to fail. Failure is a crucial part of discovery and innovation. You cannot grow unless you fail. If you do not like to fail, you tend to stick to the old methods of the past. This hinders innovation and creativity. Leaders who like to stick to the past methods often force their employees to use the old methods as well. This creates a negative influence circle and stagnates the growth of the team. The elements of curiosity and exploration die in such situations just because the leader, and in turn, the team is not ready to try new things.

A person can only learn through failure and thus, it is the responsibility of the leader to embrace failure and help his team members to accept it as well.

Leaders entirely control group outcomes

A bad leader can ruin a good group, while a good leader can make a bad group excellent. It is true that a leader plays an important role in the functioning and progress of a group, but it does not mean that the leader is responsible for the outcomes of the team. Unlike the game of chess, a team does not lose when their leader exits. A team continues to survive even if their leader is changed.

Leaders often lead groups and teams. A leader is supposed to guide, control, and help the members of a group. A good/bad leader can really influence the outcome of a team, but he or she can rarely change it. A leader can be compared to a football coach. You may bring in the best coach in the world to coach a team, but you still cannot make the team win if they do not put efforts and dedication. A team can only succeed when all the members put in efforts and show spirit.

A team is a collaboration, and it can only succeed when it works in collaboration.

While it is true that a leader is expected to be the spokesperson of a group, but leadership is a varied construct that comes in many forms. Sometimes you do not even need to be in the team to lead it. True leaders are supposed to be humble, and this humbleness can only be achieved with communication and experience.

Hogging the limelight and usurping every opportunity to shine the brightest in a group can create a negative image of your group. Many popular leaders have always been out of the limelight and still have transformed industries.

A good leader is always able to control his or her ego. He or she looks for opportunities to benefit his or her company. This does not mean that they do not possess any ego or self-interest; rather, every leader in this world has an ego and has ambition. Without ambition, a person cannot become a leader. But good leaders channel their ambition in a way that benefits their industry/team. Thus, leaders possess a dualistic nature where they are often bold and humble, and willful yet modest.

It is always recommended to remember what Harry S. Truman said:

"You can accomplish anything in life, provided that you do not mind who gets the credit."

All groups have a designated leader

Once upon a time, people used to believe that all groups need a leader who can sit at the top and guide and control everything. This belief was still prevalent a few decades ago. But now the times have changed, and people have realized that the leader does not sit at the top of the 'power pyramid'. Now there are more than one leader in a group. In fact, nowadays, many groups do not have a designated leader at all.

Gone are the days when leaders were supposed to be all-powerful and smart demigods who would guide their teams through difficult situations. People now understand that leadership is a multidimensional project. Almost all members of a group move through various dimensions of leadership throughout the day. All of us are leaders in one-way or another. It is thus necessary to use every member's talent for the benefit of the team. A team is a collaborative effort and making leadership a collaborative effort can make a significantly positive change in the functioning of the group.

Gone are the days when the leader used to be the 'lone wolf' who would isolate himself or herself from the group to appear more dynamic, bold, and powerful. People used to believe that if the leader mingled with the team, he or she would not be able to retain the 'alpha' position as others would find out about his or her weaknesses and overall attitude. The myth of pomposity and authority would shatter, and he or she would no longer be a mystical and enigmatic figure.

Everyone has a weakness, but everyone also has strengths. Nowadays, people in a group concentrate on their strengths and try to use them to counter their weaknesses. This forms a nearly unbeatable group. Every member of the group is now a leader. Good leaders now are skillful and can evoke leadership qualities from others. They are generous and bold.

Group Members Resist Leaders and Change

The world is changing rapidly, and there is an exponential growth in the world of computers. Its impact is seen on almost all facets of life, including business and entrepreneurship. While change is happening everywhere, organizational change is still difficult and will need time to happen. But if these changes do not happen soon, the organizations will collapse. Leaders are often the harbinger of changes. There is a myth doing rounds that group members resist leaders who want to bring changes.

Many seniors too blame that the employees are not ready to accept the changes. At times this may be true, but mostly it is due to the gross misunderstanding of people and overestimation. Leaders need to look at things effectively if they want to bring changes and implement them effectively. Leading requires a lot of people skills that not a lot of people possess.

Group members do not resist changes irrationally. Similarly, they do not resist leaders either. People rarely resist others if they can see that whatever the leader does will be in their best interests. Let us have a look at eight reasons due to which your group members may resist you.

Loss of status

Nobody likes to change if the change is going to harm our current situation. In administrative or organizational settings, this means that the managers, peers, employees, and even the leaders will resist change if the change means that their role will make their role obsolete. These people will believe that their leader is trying to harm them and will, therefore, resist him or her.

Changes are essential but changing it in a positive way is necessary. While it is possible to force change as a leader, you will soon find that this is not a long-term strategy. While it may show some positive results in the beginning, but in the long-term, it will end up causing more harm than benefits. If you overuse this method, you will ultimately harm your effectiveness and your employees will start to resist you.

Poorly aligned reward systems

The leaders get things that they reward. This means that the employees will show passion and dedication only if they are rewarded well. People will resist you if you do not set an active reward methodology.

Reward motivates people, and if there is no motivation, your team will stop to support you over the long term. Your system needs to change in such a way that you will be able to apply changes without resistance. Intrinsic rewards are some of the best motivators for employees. These rewards are rarely monetary. Many times, employees need mental and spiritual rewards to motivate them.

Surprise and fear of the unknown

Your employees may resist you if they do not understand your motivations and your decisions. Fear is not a great leadership tactic and surprising your employees can lead to a lot of negative flak. Your organization needs to be ready for everything, and only a leader can make them ready.

An effective communication channel needs to be established between the leader and the employees else a grapevine of rumors will form creating a serious case of miscommunication. Do not neglect your employees, or they will surely resist you.

Peer pressure

It does not matter if you are an extroverted person or an introverted person; all of us are social creatures. This means that our behavior changes significantly when we are in a group. If a few members in your group resist you, it is possible that all the other members will start resisting you as well due to peer pressure.

The need to belong to a group (within a group) is strong, especially at workplaces. While groups are great for people to feel comfortable, you should still keep an eye on the groups to keep everything under control.

Climate of mistrust

No change or progress can happen when people work in a climate of mistrust. Trust involves honesty, truth, and faith in leaders. Similarly, it involves mutual understanding and faith in the employees as well.

If you want to lead people without resistance, it is necessary to have a connection with them. If your employees trust you, they will not resist you, but if there is an environment of mutual mistrust, your group will never succeed. If you feel that there is a sense of mistrust in your workplace, it is your duty to rebuilt trust.

Trust is both extremely crucial and fragile. It can be harmed easily.

Organizational politics

It is impossible to avoid politics in the workplace. Employees, leaders, top heads, etc. all indulge in workplace politics. Employees may often believe that politics can hinder their progress. They may feel that the leader may misguide them for his or her benefit. This is, again, a classic example of miscommunication and mismanagement. If the communication channel between the leader and the employees is healthy, then there will be no problem between the leaders and the employees.

Fear of failure

Employees and subordinates are often afraid of failure. It is possible that they may resist their leader if they feel that their leader will lead them to fail. They may be worried that if they follow the path shown by their leader, they may enter a world where they cannot succeed.

Fear motivates people, but it can also cause a variety of problems that may lead to failure. If you want to be successful and want your employees to respect you, it is recommended to avoid using fear as a motivator.

Faulty Implementation Approach

Knowledge can be divided into two parts: data and communications. You may have a lot of data, but if you do not know how to communicate it, then your data becomes useless. What you do is important, but how you do it is crucial. Misplaced communication can lead to undue resistance, especially if new changes are brought in in an insensitive manner. Timings are important as well.

Your employees may understand what you want, but they might not appreciate the way in which you want to do the object. You need to think of proper strategies and ideas if you want to implement a change without resistance.

Thus, it is clear that employees do not resist change irrationally. If you can prove to them that you, the leader, is working for their benefit, then they will support you unconditionally.

Final Thoughts on Leadership

Leaders are responsible for their teams and ultimately, the world. Leaders have the opportunity to act in a creative way rather than following an old, patterned, and highly reactive way. Leaders can truly bring in a lot of positive changes in the world if they know their potential and understand the strengths of their group.

A leader needs to be dynamic and active. He or she also needs to be inclusive and understanding because every member of the group possesses some talent and skills. For instance, think that your team is trying to open a huge lock with many keys. Some of the keys are gigantic while some are tiny, but the lock cannot open unless all the keys are inserted in it. Thus, even the tiniest key holds the same amount of respect and importance as the biggest one. A good leader understands this and helps his or her team to grow.

Discarding the myths associated with leadership can help you become bold. It can help you find new horizons and definitions of leadership. It will encourage you and your team to become the very best. Ultimately, leadership is a complex and dynamic concept. There is no one size fits all solution. Every leader has his or her own style, attitude, and approach towards things what is common among all the leaders, though are the myths, which need to be destroyed. Once these are destroyed, you can surely rise to the top along with your team.

Chapter Two: Contexts/Your Position and Making the Most of It

Organizations

Meaning

An entrepreneur is responsible for organizing a variety of factors, including the capital, labor, machinery, etc. He or she does this to channelize these into productive activities. The product travels through a lot of channels and agencies and finally reaches the customers. Business activities can be divided into different functions, and each function is assigned to different individuals as well.

A single person cannot achieve a common business goal; various individuals must come together and make it a success.

The organization is this framework where individuals can read come together and divide their responsibilities, duties, and functions. Management is responsible for combining various business activities in the form of predetermined goals.

The contemporary business system is highly complex. To ensure its place in the business world, a business needs to run smoothly. Many jobs need to be performed by many different individuals who are suitable for them. All these authorities need to be grouped into different groups according to functions. The authority and responsibilities are fixed according to their functions.

Concepts of Organization

There are two concepts of organization:

Static Concept

In this, the organization is a structure, a network, or an entity composed of specified relationships. Thus, in the static form, the organization is a group of people who come together and form a formal relationship so that they can achieve a common objective. It is more focused on the positions and not the individuals.

Dynamic Concept

In this concept, the organization is considered to be an ongoing and continuous process. In this concept, an organization is a process in which people, work, and systems are organized. It is related to the process of determining activities that are required to achieve a goal. It also involves the arrangement of these activities into groups so that they can be assigned. This concept considers the organization to be an open and adaptive system. It is not a closed system, unlike the static concept. In a dynamic concept, individuals are the most important aspect.

Management

Management is the art (and science) of getting people together to acquire the same goal using coordination and integration of all the available sources. Management includes all the task and activities that are performed to achieve a goal. These activities include leading, planning, controlling, and organizing.

Management involves decision-making, planning, leading, organizing, and motivating and controlling human resources. It also involves planning and controlling physical and informational resources of an organization to help it to reach the top in an effective and efficient method.

In a broader sense, management is like:

Management is an Economic Factor

I asked an economist; management is one of the major factors responsible for production along with capital, land, and labor. Increase in industrialization is directly responsible for the growth of management. Managerial resources try to decide on profitability and productivity. In such firms, executive development is more necessary as it is directly responsible for rapid progress.

Management is a System of Authority

From the point of view of an administrator, management is like a system of authority. Management was first developed as an authoritarian philosophy in ancient times. Later with time, it developed into a more paternalistic theory. After the paternalistic form, it transformed into constitutional management in which consistent policies and procedures are the major concerns. Nowadays, it has transformed into a more democratic and participatory form.

Modern management is a synthetic combination of all the four approaches mentioned above.

Management is a Class and Status System

Sociologists often refer to management as a class-and-status system. Relationships in modern society are becoming more and more complex, which is why, nowadays, managers are often supposed to be highly educated and brainy. If anyone wants to enter into this class of leaders, you need to be highly educated and earn a lot of knowledge as well. Your education and skills are more important than your political and familial connections. According to some scholars, this is 'Managerial Revolution'.

Management is also a highly individualistic affair, and some people may view it from a different point of view. But the ultimate motive of management is to reach a goal in an efficient and effective manner.

Feature of Management

As said above, management is the process of reaching and setting goals in an efficient and effective manner. This process has certain features or qualities. In this section, let us have a look at these qualities one by one.

Management and Group Efforts

Management is usually associated with group efforts. While people may manage personal affairs individually, in groups, management becomes universal. In every organization, groups are necessary to achieve goals. It has been proven that goals can be achieved with ease if groups are formed.

Management and Purposefulness

Management does not exist without purpose. Management deals closely with the achievement of goals and objectives. The success of management can be measured by comparing the extent to which the goals are achieved. Management is an effective way of achieving goals.

Management and the Efforts of Others

Management is often defined as accomplishing things with the help of others. An organization cannot survive only on the hard work of the manager. Engineers, accountants, salesmen, system analysts, and various other employees all need to put in a lot of work to make an organization successful. All their work needs to be integrated with the work of the manager.

Management and Goal-orientedness

Management is all about achieving a preset goal. Successful managers have a desire for accomplishment. Such managers are aware of where and when to start a process and how to keep it moving as well. Managers are highly goal-oriented, and they know how to influence their group members to become goal-oriented as well.

Management is Indispensable

Management is indispensable, and it cannot be substituted or replaced by anything else. Many people believed that with the advent of computers, managers would become obsolete; however, it was soon proven that computers could only help managers but cannot replace them. Computers can help to widen the vision of the managers and make their insights sharp as well. They allow managers to make decisions quickly. The computer allows managers to conduct analysis that is beyond the normal analytical capacities of a normal human being. In reality, the computer can neither work on itself nor can it pass any judgment. Even the advent of virtual reality and artificial intelligence cannot replace managers. The manager will always be relevant because he or she can use his or her imagination and provide judgment as well.

Management is Intangible

Management is often known as unseen force, and its presence is present in the efforts as well as motivation present in the employees. It is also seen in the productivity and discipline of the group.

Management and Better Life

A manager is responsible for a lot of things. He or she can improve the work atmosphere and can also stimulate group members to perform and work better. He or she can instill a sense of hope in the group members.

Group

Man is a social animal who loves to live in a group. This group can be society, club, family, college, institute, college etc. This instinct is also found in animals such as leopards, elephants, lions, sheep, etc. Leaders are the people who lead the groups. Leaders are supposed to have commitment, vision, and drive to achieve the mission of the group. Team leadership is essentially the management of a group. The leader should be able to inspire and motivate the members of the team. The leader should also be adaptable and flexible.

Group Leadership for Project Management

A project is a particular task undertaken by a group. It can be anything such as software development, construction of a building, managing social parties etc. In the initial phases of the project, a plan is necessary. A plan should include budget, available resources, goal, members, and motive.

Teamwork

The team leader should be able to lead the members of the team effectively. All the individual members of the team should get an environment that is suitable for efficient and effective work. Following is a list of things that are necessary for individual group members.

- Equal opportunities for growth and development for all members of the group.
o Safe atmosphere to work. This includes physical as well as social and mental safety.
- Respect each member of the group. Respect given is respect gained.
- If conflict ever arises in the group, it should be solved amicably.
o Regular meetings should be conducted to monitor the progress of the group and should solve the problems as well.
- If a failure occurs, it should be analyzed with proper meetings.
- If success occurs, it should be celebrated.
- A leader should always try to get honest feedback from the group members.
o Once the feedback is received, it should be analyzed, and corrective measures should be undertaken.

Self-leadership

What is self-leadership?

Self-leadership can be defined as the capability to gain the motivation and direction that can positively influence your performance and work. It is related to mastery and personal excellence. Self-leadership is closely associated with self-confidence, self-efficacy, and your self-beliefs. The confidence and ability to complete goals and tasks is closely related to self-leadership. Self-leadership allows you to become your best self and helps you develop a personal brand as well. It makes you compete with yourself, which can help you to achieve your professional as well as personal goals.

Importance of self-leadership in the current world

Today's world is highly competitive. It changes significantly almost every minute. This means that you need to be unique and remarkable if you want to stand out from the crowd. You need to communicate in an effective, clear, and bold manner so that other people can understand your ideas.

If you want to be a leader, you should create foundations that can help you to display your leadership skills. The team is responsible for the direction, commitment, and alignment. It is true that leadership and self-leadership are different, but they are complementary to each other.

How to achieve self-leadership?

Achieving self-leadership leads to a lot of dedication and passion. Here are some tips that can help you to achieve self-leadership effectively.

Purpose in Life

A self-aware leader should always ask himself or herself a question, 'what is the purpose of my existence?' Without a purpose in life, you are left at the mercy of your fate. Having a clear direction and a sense of purpose keeps you on track and allows you to develop strategies that can help you your goals.

Blind Spots

Blind spots are the aspects of your personality that you are unaware of including feelings and values. You need to become aware of these blind spots. This awareness requires a lot of courage and boldness. It involves getting feedback from others, often from your subordinates. This will help you become more self-aware and ultimately successful as well.

Character Building

Personal character is composed of behavior and mental characteristics. This personal character sets you apart. It displays moral potency and is related to moral efficacy, moral ownership, and moral courage. Character is related to your integrity. Integrity refers to the set of characteristics that define your trustworthiness and credibility. A good leader is supposed to be consistent with their values and promises. Being consistent with your values allows you to be reputable. Reputation is necessary for good leadership; it can even be your most powerful asset.

Ethics and Integrity

If you want to become a self-leader, you need to become selfless. You should be ethical and should possess integrity, as well. You should be fair, honest, and diverse. Ethics are essential and should not be left to chance.

Family

Families are quite similar to organizations, specifically community organizations. There are many different kinds of families, including old fashioned, extended families, modern nuclear families, single parents, childless parents etc. All these variants are commonly seen in the modern world. Almost all these families and their leaders are based around the same principles of leadership. By applying these principles, you can bring a lot of happiness and success for your family.

Importance of leadership in families

There exist many ways in which leadership can help in the maintenance of the family. A family should always support the development and growth of the family members. A good leader can help family members grow in a holistic manner. A good family leader is not only concerned about the materialistic needs of the family members, but they are also concerned with the emotional needs of the family members as well.

Balance

Leadership is essential if you want to balance the different needs of the family members. It is true that the needs of one member may dominate at certain times, for instance, in the case of injury or illness, but with time the normal function of the family must be restored.

Generally, children are the priority of the family as compared to especially. This is especially true in the case of parents.

Another common problem that causes an imbalance in the family is when one adult dominates the whole family. For instance, if the mother (the head of the family) forces her family to live a strange lifestyle of denial and isolation, the family will become miserable. The imbalance is especially bad for children of the family.

Common Goal

Leadership in the family allows setting a common goal for the family. This allows the family to be healthy, happy, and satisfied. Like any other organization, a family needs a vision as well. A family needs to have a mission or a purpose to which its members can subscribe.

This mission is generally the successful growth and development of children.

Creating Leadership in The Family

In regular families, leadership is often owned by the parents. Sometimes this leadership can be held jointly by both the parents and sometimes it can be held by one of the two parents as well. It depends on the parent how he or she approaches leadership. It depends on the leader how he or she handles the responsibilities.

It is necessary to remember that families work like regular organizations as well. The family leader can achieve respect, success, and authority if he or she follows the rules of leadership. The leader of the family should be able to develop the same leadership skills that are required by other leaders. These qualities include open-mindedness, communication skills, fairness, integrity, commitment, and generosity.

CEO

A CEO or the Chief Executive Officer of any organization is a multi-faceted leader who needs to possess a variety of qualities. They are supposed to have many different skills and knowledge.

Initially, organizations would employ those leaders who had pertinent administration experience. Today, they are happy to take chances on leaders who bring distinctive ranges of abilities to the table and utilize those to enable the organization to grow in the modern world.

No one is a born leader. With ample practice and dedication, everyone can learn how to be a great leader. With dedication and practice, a person can gain the skills necessary to be a great leader.

Inspiring people to do things

A leader should be able to light a fire of inspiration in the mind of his or her employees. He or she needs to learn how to communicate in such a way that will inspire people to do their jobs in an efficient manner. CEOs and other bosses need to understand that connecting with employees leads to efficient work and good work ethic. Honesty begets honesty.

Rapidity

As mentioned above, the world is undergoing continuous and rapid change. Change is present in every nook and cranny of the world. The corporate world is undergoing rapid changes in almost all aspects. There are technological changes, financial changes, social changes, economic changes, societal changes, etc. All these changes impact the corporate world and are rapidly causing problems. For instance the problems that were solved over the past few years have now returned with a vengeance. The old solutions have become obsolete. Thus, a leader needs to understand the methodology of change and learn to change with the times as well. He or she should be able to lead his group toward adaptation, change and growth.

Emotional Intelligence

Emotional intelligence as a concept has been discussed in detail in the last chapter of this book.

School Can't make you a great leader. A leader needs to learn their job themselves. Unlike other jobs, leaders are allowed to make very few errors. A successful leader possesses essential skills, such as trustworthiness, vision, acumen, high emotional intelligence, etc. These skills can only be developed with time, practice, and dedication. Good leaders are often great visionaries and can use these skills to help motivate their team.

Chapter Three: Behavioral and Style Theories/ Leadership Development Methods and Tips

In this section, let's take a look at the various styles of developing leadership and how leadership is closely related to other business tactics.

Allegiance and Leadership

Many people feel that loyalty has become a rare commodity in today's world. Backstabbing has become a common phenomenon, and everyone is trying to step on the other person just to reach the top. People have become self-centered and care about nothing but their own benefits. Loyalty and leadership are closely related. A leader cannot succeed if he or she is not loyal to his or her employees and vice versa.

Loyalty and trust can be used in many different ways, but it is also possible to misuse them. Relationships are being degenerated almost every day in today's world, and it is no wonder that loyalty has become an elusive trait. If a leader wants to become a great leader, he or she needs to create an atmosphere where loyalty, trust, and faith hold the center stage. These three factors need to be the rules with no exceptions.

Relationships are, in a way, the currency of leadership. Leaders need to know that loyalty can help their group to grow. Loyalty and leadership go hand in hand. If a leader fails to understand this simple fact, they will not survive in this world. There are many different things that make a leader successful, but loyalty is always the common denominator in all these equations. Loyalty is a two-way street; if the leader is loyal towards the employees, the employees will be loyal to the leader and the leaders agenda. You will receive what you give and vice versa.

It is crucial for leaders to understand the difference between trust-based loyalty and fear-based loyalty. One of them is real and permanent while the other one is fake and temporary.

If people are loyal to you just because you are a leader, then this kind of loyalty will always disappear. If people are loyal to you because you have earned their respect and faith, then their loyalty will never go away.

Being a team manager is a great duty. You can never be a great leader if you believe that being feared is a sign of trust and honor. Employees should respect you, but should never be scared of you. Imposing fear is easy, but earning respect takes a long time. A fear-based style of leadership will never allow trust, loyalty, creativity, innovation, and talent. It will always crush these crucial traits. Fear stifles and hinders people, while loyalty promotes them.

A leader who uses fear-based tactics to control people will always fail. This is because: his or her employees will not give their best performance. When things get tough or when other options are available, the employees will run away and leave the leader alone. If a leader believes that instilling fear in someone's mind is a great way to control them, then you are not a leader; rather you are a tyrannical bully. You will never earn loyalty from your employees.

It is necessary to remember that great people do not consider them to be the masters of the universe; rather they see themselves as inspirational teachers, catalysts, servants, and team builders. There is a huge difference between a leader and a dictator. For instance, the teachers who can inspire students, who can encourage the students to follow their passions, and who can challenge the students in a positive way are the best teachers. If the teacher in a highly dominating way and is too proud, his or her students will despise him or her. He or she will not be appreciated as a great leader.

You may be confused about how to know whether your employees respect you or are they afraid of you.

Tips to Judge

There are five simple tips that can help you to make your judgment.

Yes-men

Leaders who use fear-based tactics to control other people often surround themselves with like-minded people. If they cannot find like-minded people, they tend to surround themselves with a bunch of people who share their views in a vacuum. Everyone likes praise, but false praise instils a false sense of security, which can ultimately lead to a lot of problems. Great leaders will always value the opinion of their group members even if the opinion goes against their decision. Good leaders always keep their ideas open for scrutiny and debate. They encourage their group members to discuss the decisions and ideas.

Interaction

The leaders who use fear-based tactics to control people often avoid interacting with their employees. If you feel that your employees do not interact with you or seek your advice, then it is possible that they do not respect you. They do not treat your decisions as important and believe that your ideas are useless. They may also be afraid of you belittling them. In a fear-based scenario, the employees may think that there is no use of talking to the superiors, so why bother. This lack of interaction is often a result of fear.

Feedback

In the first section, we saw how a good leader puts his or her ideas for scrutiny. Similarly, a good leader also puts himself or herself up for scrutiny. A great leader must subject himself or herself for a 360-review process if he or she ever wants to succeed. Scrutiny allows for developmental opportunities, and it allows people to grow professionally and personally. When you put yourself up for scrutiny, you will not get 100% positive responses. But it is necessary to accept all kinds of responses and evaluate them. This will allow becoming the best version of yourself. If you use fear-based tactics, then you will only receive positive comments, which will be insincere flattery. Flattery is a sign of dishonesty.

Effectiveness

If you cannot retain people, then you are not an effective leader. An effective and great leader has loyal employees who would not leave him or her without any reason. A leader who uses fear-based tactics to lead people will never have a satisfactory team. Their team will consist of people who are not passionate about their work.

Poor Performance

Employees who respect their leaders will always perform better than the employees who are scared of their leaders. Leaders who tend to control and command people with the help of fear rarely do well. If you think that your company is not growing, then it is necessary to check your leadership style. Constant evaluation can help a leader to grow.

Question and Evaluation

Imagine, if your employees hold an election, will you be re-elected once again by a landslide or will they dethrone you immediately? If you choose the latter option, then you need to evaluate your decisions and leadership styles. Things that have been earned like trust, loyalty, and friendship will always outlast the things that have been snatched or forced. People will always stand by you if they truly respect you.

Traits of Leaders Who Inspire Loyalty

Nowadays, modern workers are less likely to retain their jobs and remain at the same company for a long time. People transition from one job to another all the time, but this not because loyalty has become obsolete. Rather the value of loyalty has gone up significantly because now it has become a rare commodity. Many leaders and organizations still try to instill loyalty in their group members. Here are some traits of leaders who inspire loyalty in others.

Authenticity

The leaders who are authentic and honest will always find their subordinates to be loyal and honest as well. No one likes working for fake people. Nowadays the younger generation will look for a new job instead of suffering under a fake person who has little to no respect for them. This means that authenticity has now become a precious factor. People trust authentic leaders because they are accountable for. They act the same way in front of their superiors and subordinates as well. They do not change their 'colours' according to the situation.

Service

The leaders who believe that their job is to guide and motivate the lives of their group members are great leaders, and they will always find loyal followers. For such leaders, team members are more than mere workers; for them, they are real people with real goals. Great leaders understand that they can help these people to achieve their goals.

These leaders try to find the purpose and the meaning behind their employees' goals that can help them to motivate them. Success is a relative term. A group cannot succeed unless everyone participates. A successful group is a group in which every person is trying to grow.

Professional Development of the Employees

Your subordinates will not be loyal to you if you are not willing to mentor them. The best leaders always try to find ways and methods through which their staff members can develop not only professionally but personally as well. The employees who believe that they can develop professionally under a leader will always be loyal to him or her. If the employees act disloyal, then it is due to their leaders not providing them with enough opportunities to grow.

If you want to be a great leader, it is recommended to find opportunities through which you can train and challenge your employees. Normally such resources are available in every company, but if they are not, try to bring them from the outside. Developing and cultivating the talent and skills of your employees will ultimately prove beneficial to the organization.

Display of Trust

Great leaders try to push their group members out of their comfort zone while supporting them thoroughly. If the leader is confident, his or her followers will be confident as well. Such members will be ready to accept any challenge, thanks to the trust and support of their leaders. But this trust cannot be verbal only. You need to display trust through your actions as well. Employees who understand that their leader will support them even if they take on bigger challenges will always be loyal to the leader.

Ideas

Good leaders are always open about their beliefs and ideas. Such leaders often serve as an inspiration to their group members. These leaders display their ideas, thoughts, and decisions openly. If the leader can display what they want in an honest way, their group member will understand the passion of their leader.

Great leaders are unafraid of being wrong or rather being proved wrong. They do not care if they win or lose, but they believe that a healthy debate is necessary for better decisions. They are energetic and understand that if they want the group to succeed, they will have to work together. A despotic leader will never get loyal followers.

They Always Pitch In

Inspiring leaders always try to work with people whom they are supposed to oversee. This creates a sense of camaraderie between the workers and their leader. It also shows how the leader does not consider any work or project to be less important or useless. Nothing is beneath a great leader. If an emergency arises, a great leader will arrive first at the scene and will try to rectify it immediately. They don't expect others to do the tasks that they themselves will not do.

Interest in Employees Lives

People who inspire loyalty are often interested in the lives of others. They can share a lot of information about their group members because they are genuinely interested in their wellbeing. This includes not only their professional life but also their personal interests, family, friends, etc. If you want your employees to be loyal, you need to know them as people. While personal and professional lives are two separate things, both of them influence each other. Supporting and helping an employee in his or her personal crisis will definitely help him or her in their professional life.

People Follow Because They Want To

Leaders are supposed to be the heroes of the corporate world. They encourage us to take risks that we would never take otherwise. They help their groups to produce results. In the corporate world, good leadership can make or break a business. It is no wonder that people spend so much money and time trying to develop leaders.

But often, while trying to understand and grasp the skills necessary for leadership, people tend to forget that there are two facets of the leadership equation. A leader requires more than exceptional talent to attract followers. It has now become significantly difficult to find followers in the modern world. The major problem behind this is that most managerial programs and literature are related only to the qualities of the leader. These texts believe that if you are charismatic, you will attract followers. This is a myth, as a person needs to have a variety of skills to attract followers. Leaders and employees are equally driven by their passions.

There are two motivations behind a person to follow someone; they are rational and irrational. Rational followers are conscious. They understand why they should follow a person. Some major reasons why a person will become a rational follower include status, money, power, or connections. Irrational followers, however, have motives that lie beyond the conventional word. These motivations are often due to powerful images and emotions. These images and emotions are often a result of the subconscious.

It was Sigmund Freud, the father of psychoanalysis who first tried to evaluate followers' unconscious motivation to work. By practicing psychoanalysis for years together, he was confused to see that his patients kept falling in love with him. While most of these patients identified as women, many others identified as men as well. Freud soon realized that this infatuation was not a result of his personal qualities; rather, it was because the patients related him to a past figure in their lives. So, some people related him to their father or uncle, etc. Thus, people were transferring their feeling of love for their parents onto Freud. Freud believed that this phenomenon was universal. He believed that this is the reason why many people choose spouses or partners who are like our parents.

According to Freud, this dynamic is known as 'transference'. Transference is considered to be one of the most important discoveries of Freud. According to Freud, a patient would be 'cured' once they understood their transference. But even today, identifying transference is a difficult objective. It is still considered to be a major goal of psychoanalysis.

Not all transference is positive. For instance, if the employee sees his employer acting like a snob or being rude towards someone, the employee will emulate the employer's behaviour. Transference is not permanent, for instance, an employee may continue to emulate the leader, but if his or her expectations are not met, he or she may end the transference process.

Just because you are a leader does not mean that your employees will follow you or your orders. Anyone can become a leader, but to become a successful leader, you need to work hard to earn the confidence, trust, and respect of people. Only then will you become popular, and people will start taking you seriously.

Anyone can hone their skills to become a great and popular leader. All you need is dedication, passion, and practice. With determination and practice, you will soon become a popular leader.

Tips to Become A Popular Leader

Here are a few things that you should practice to become a popular leader.

Give Respect, Gain Respect

Being respectful is easy when the situation and the person is motivated and mature, but this is rarely the case. Leaders often need to deal with difficult people who will often end up eating your patience and time with strange ideas and requests. Similarly, some employees may get on your nerves as well. In such situations, it becomes difficult to maintain your calm and continue in a respectful demeanor.

True respect does not depend on the situation or the person. True respect is the belief that all human beings are inherently worthy of being respected; this includes people who test your patience as well. This means that you need to treat people in a way that will preserve their as well as your dignity and honour.

When you act respectfully towards every person you interact with, you create an environment of love and caring that soon enveloped your workplace. This atmosphere encourages employees, leaders, and everyone else to treat each other and the clients in a respectful manner. Remember that your employees will always try to imitate you, so if you act respectful, they will act respectfully as well.

Communication

Great leaders understand that communication is the key to leadership. Communicating your ideas in a clear yet concise manner is necessary if you want to avoid any misunderstandings or confusions. While the main focus of communication is to deliver messages, there are many other factors that make communication so crucial for the corporate world.

Communication should always be informative and efficient. It should be used in such a way that it should motivate, inspire, and persuade others. When leaders communicate in a particular way, they can truly enjoy the true results of good communication.

Be Generous

Generosity is often confused with monetary generosity. But this is just one form of generosity. While keeping your employees happy by giving them frequent bonuses, gifts, and promotions is a great way to display generosity, you can display it in various other ways as well.

One of the easiest ways to display generosity is by encouraging and praising your employees liberally. Always praise your employees when they deserve it. Similarly, be gracious if they ever commit a mistake. It also means that you should let go of some control and let others take more responsibilities.

Do not expect something in return while being generous. Try to be self-less, and you will instantly become popular.

Display Your Passion

Passion is contagious. When the leader is excited and passionate about a task, his or her employees will feel enthusiastic as well. But just being passionate will not help you to get others excited; you need to display your passion and enthusiasm.

Expressing your passion will allow your employees to understand how invested you are in a task. They will understand how passionate you are about the task and how important it is for you. By looking at your passion, they will understand that what they are doing is worthwhile and that their work is not useless.

Be Humble

Humbleness is a great way to influence people and become a popular leader. But sometimes humbleness can be confused with being a pushover. Do not let people walk all over you. Be humble but be bold as well. You should take responsibility for your mistakes and should also accept the fact that there are some activities that your employees can do better than you. Nobody is perfect.

Humble leaders are not only more effective, but they are better liked as well. Learning and development take a lot of hard work. Failure is the first step to success. Leaders who can overcome their fears and can move forward are considered to be bold and humble. People love such leaders because they show humane qualities.

Take Responsibility for Your Decisions

Making tough decisions in the times of adversity is one of the most important traits of great leaders. Great leaders will always accept the results of their decisions, whether negative or positive. Even the leader makes a poor decision; he or she needs to accept the result. Accusing others of your own fault will make you an infamous leader.

A great leader should not be afraid of making decisions. He should also be able to take risks. Seeking opportunities and taking responsibilities are two other traits that make great leaders so popular.

Show courage

Displaying courage in times of difficulty is one of the best ways to inspire others. It is impossible to find a person who is not scared of anything. Even the greatest leaders feel afraid from time to time. Leaders are often scared of competition, risks, failure, and similar circumstances. But inspiring leaders will always try to ignore and face their fear and will display courage. Fear produces a lot of energy. This energy can be harnessed and converted into courage. Using this courage, great leaders move ahead and face their fears gallantly. Courage is influential, and group members often feel bold if their leader is courageous.

Courageous leaders understand the importance of their team. They understand that they cannot do anything without their teams.

It is true that becoming a popular leader and getting followers is a difficult task. Not all people can do it naturally, but these skills are not innate, and you can learn them as well. With time and practice, you can learn how to be a popular leader. Just practice the above steps religiously, and you will soon become a great leader.

People Development

One of the most important things that a leader can do for his or her employees is by helping them to develop. Developing employees professionally and personally can help the company to develop as well. When employees are developed, they become more productive, smarter, and bolder. They start performing in a better way. This way, the group will develop. A leader becomes great when he or she changes the lives of other people. Developing people is the best way to change the lives of people.

If you do not know how to mentor and motivate people, here are some tips that can help you get started.

Charity Begins at Home

Before you decide or begin to improve and develop others, you need to develop yourself. If you don't develop others before yourself, you will end up looking like a hypocrite. People will not consider you to be a genuine mentor or leader who is interested in the development of his employees. Employees often follow their leaders, and it is thus necessary to become a good role model if you want your employees to develop. Developing your skills will also help you to become smarter and bolder, and you will be able to develop others in a far more effective way.

Trust and Mutual Respect

Employees should understand that by recommending development strategies, you are not insulting them. Many people avoid visiting developmental seminars because they are afraid that their weaknesses will be exposed. You can avoid this pitfall by building a rapport with them. Try to connect with them and create an atmosphere of trust and faith. Make them understand that you are interested in their development and wellbeing.

Learning Opportunities

Employee development does not happen in the annual review. Similarly, it does not happen in the HR department either. It needs a lot of work, as it is a prolonged process. There are many learning opportunities spread out throughout the office hours.

For instance, project check-ins, interactions, talks, and meetings, etc. are all great learning opportunities through which you can develop your employees.

Ask Questions

While dictating is the norm, people rarely perform when they are merely dictated. Dictation rarely creates passionate and involved employees. If you want to involve your employees- ask good questions. By asking frequent and good questions to the employees, you will allow them opportunities through which they will be forced to think on their own and come up with solutions. This will help them learn and develop.

Learn How to Delegate

A lot of leaders often spend the time of work that they should not be doing. It is necessary to learn how to let off responsibilities so that others can take them over. Delegating tasks and responsibilities on your employees will not only make your schedule freer, but it will also provide your employees with opportunities to develop. Thus, this is a win-win situation. The only thing you need to remember is that the results will not be the same. It is possible that your employees may fail at first, but even the failure will help them to develop. Ultimately, they may start to perform even better than you do.

Stretch Assignments

The two best ways to develop and learn in the corporate world are stretch assignments and job change. While job change is not always possible, stretch assignments can help your employees to develop significantly. As a leader, you can find a variety of opportunities for your employees according to their needs. Avoid picking the most qualified person for a job, as this will make them stagnant; instead, pick a person who can learn a lot from such assignments. This will help them develop, and ultimately, you will end up with a team in which everyone will be equally skilled and talented.

Networking Introductions

It is impossible to succeed in the corporate world if you are not well connected. Managers are often well connected. They should use these connections to introduce their subordinates with other people. This will allow them to connect their employees with mentors, experts, and models. Expanding an employee's network can help them to become more skilled and talented. This will also remind the employees that you are not the only person who can help them grow. It will also help you to grow, as you too will cement your relationship with your employee and your contacts.

Feedback

Nobody is perfect, and everyone has a weak spot or two. A bad leader will confront their employees and insult them for their weaknesses. A good leader, however, will try to be tactful and will explain the employee his or her weakness in a calm way. The leader will give well-worded feedback that can help the employee to rectify his or her mistake and avoid it in the future as well.

Organizational Politics and Culture

Politics is often considered to be a dirty field, but it is impossible to escape it in the corporate world. Your staff needs to understand this and look at politics from a positive point of view. They should understand how to navigate office culture. A great way to make your employees politically savvy is using role-playing. Through this method, you can teach the employees the in's and out of the office politics and culture.

Spend Money

Nothing is free in this world, and if you want your employees to grow and develop, you should be ready to invest in them. Some great way to enrich your employees include coaches, training, conferences, workshops, etc. These tangible resources require tangible investment in the form of money. A good training program can work wonders with the employees. It will also help your employees to understand that you appreciate them and are ready to spend real money on their development.

Chapter Four: Leadership Development Methods and Tips

Significant Leadership Behaviors and Attitude

Listening and Communication

Communication is something that sets us apart from all other animals. Thanks to our skills in communication, we can talk, lead and participate in a group. Leaders need to have excellent communication and listening skills if they want to succeed. In this section, let us have a look at some communication skills.

Listening

Listening is perhaps the most important skill a leader can possess. The ability to listen and act upon it is essential for everyone who wants to succeed. Professional listening skills comprise of listening to the message, listening for emotions hidden behind the messages, and understanding the relevant questions regarding the message.

Listening for message includes hearing the facts correctly and understanding them carefully. This includes listening to the messages without any prejudice and prejudgment. You should not be distracted by any thoughts or ideas while listening to the message. Many times, people only concentrate on the words of a message and fail to understand the emotions behind them. This leads to incorrect understanding. You should be able to hear the signs of emotions, especially the changing intonations and rising (or lowering) pitch.

Complimenting

People who believe that employees only work for money do not understand the human psyche. Along with money, people also like to be praised and noticed for their work.

Compliments are especially effective when they are paid in writing, and when they are relevant to the situation. A written compliment stays with the person for a long time, and the person can read it multiple times as well.

This method is great for managers, leaders, supervisors, and everyone else who wants to appreciate their colleagues.

Delegating Tasks Clearly

When you plan a task, you should ideally plan 'what', 'who', 'where', 'when', 'how', and 'why'. These six things should be in your mind when you explain something to another person as well. Explaining the 'why' or the reason behind a task is essential, especially when related to deadlines. It is possible that the employee may not understand that their task is a small part of a grand task. When they understand this, they will work with a new passion and zeal.

Managing Meetings

Understanding how to manage meetings is an essential communication skill that a leader needs to understand. A meeting should be 'good' from the point of view of not only the leader but all other participants as well.

Understanding the value of time of all the participants will allow you to understand the worth of the meeting. If ever you believe that a topic can be discussed and informed using just an email, then conducting a meeting for it is useless.

The purpose of the meeting should always be useful and relevant for everyone. Often you can conduct a proper discussion using just email. Just ask open-ended questions that demand answers. This method works great with employees who are introverts. They may have brilliant ideas, but they may not present them in meetings due to their introversion.

Positive Verbal and Non-Verbal Communication

Communication is not just about words; it is about your emotions, your behavior, your gestures, and your movements as well. Employees pay close attention to their leaders. They analyze and many times, reciprocate and replicate the behaviors of their employers. For instance, if a leader receives bad news and acts violently or too emotionally, the employees will lose respect for the leader. But if the leader acts composed and accepts the news gracefully, he or she will become immensely popular.

Remember to keep a simple smile on your face when you greet someone. This will make you appear courteous.

Communication skills are necessary if you want to succeed in business and want to become a successful leader. The above strategies will help you become a great communicator and in turn, will help you become a great leader as well.

Assertiveness

Many people confuse assertiveness with confidence. Both of these skills are essential if you want to become a successful leader. Assertiveness is a mixture of aggressiveness and passiveness. If you act passive while expressing your views, people will believe that you are submissive. But if you act too aggressive while expressing your ideas, people will think that you are either too hostile or a bully.

Learning to become assertive will help you to express your views without being too aggressive or passive. You will be able to put forward your ideas without offending or confusing anyone.

In this section, let us have a look at some ways that can help you become more assertive.

Understand assertiveness

Before becoming assertive, you need to understand what assertiveness is. Being assertive is considered to be an interpersonal skill that allows you to be confident and bold without hindering the ideas of others or disrespecting them. Assertiveness means that you do not act in a passive or aggressive manner. You act with honesty and directness instead. Assertiveness allows you to be confident and calm while presenting your ideas.

Keep your communication style inline

Assertiveness is closely related to your communication style and methodology. You need to learn how to be respectful towards people and how to communicate this respect as well.

You can show respect through your words, intonations, pitch, gestures, and body movements. Pay close attention to your body language while talking. Your body language and your words should match. People are not mind readers and thus if you want to convey something, do so clearly. Do not expect them to read your mind. When you make a request or present a preference, do so with immense confidence. Always stand or sit straight and smile while keeping a neutral face. Looking people in the eye is a great way of being confident and assertive.

Understand and accept differences

No two people are alike, and everyone is unique and different in their own way. This means that everyone will have a different point of view, and opinions as well. Never be dismissive of anyone's point of view. Just state your own opinion and try to understand the other person's ideas. Never become angry, frustrated, or sad just because somebody else has different ideas. Never interrupt while someone else is talking. Be respectful.

Speak simply and directly

Speaking in a simple and matter of fact tone is necessary while being assertive. You shouldn't imply things or make other people feel awkward. Speaking the truth should not make others uncomfortable. Always be straightforward, direct, simple, and concise. Remember, less is more, especially when you are asserting yourself. Avoid long-winded explanations and keep your requests and ideas to the point.

Exercise the power of "I."

There is no 'I' in a team, but there is an 'I' in assertiveness. If you want to be assertive without being hostile use 'I' statements frequently. Use starters such as 'I believe...', 'I think...', 'I feel...' etc. Do not use aggressive starters such as 'you never...' or 'you always....' These lines can often cause other people problems and leave them frustrated. A frustrated person will not want to have a conversation with you. 'I' statements will allow you to be assertive without alienating others.

Stay calm

Great leaders rarely lose their modicum and calm. Excitement can often come across as aggression. It is necessary to be calm and cool while expressing your ideas. This will make you appear more confident and will help all the other people relax and listen to you carefully. Maintain a positive body language and eye contact while talking to people. Your breathing and intonations should be normal and composed. Be present with each other.

A calm mind leads to a calm speech that in turn leads to calm action. This will keep you and your colleagues composed.

Set boundaries

Boundaries are important, as they are your personal rules. You should have some personal limits that you should avoid crossing. This is true in the case of assertiveness as well. Never allow people to talk over you, but never act like a bully either. Setting such boundaries will help you to understand when to say yes and how to say no.

Assertiveness is a skill that will take time and practice. You should cultivate and hone it slowly. Practice the above techniques every day, and soon you will become more confident, bold, and assertive.

Authenticity

Authenticity makes a leader 'real' and genuine. Authentic Leadership as a theory is still in its infancy; however, people now accept that authenticity can help leaders become more secure, strong, and bold. A practical approach to authenticity can help you become a great leader. There are many different qualities that can help a person become an authentic leader. If a person displays these qualities, their employees will respond in a positive and comprehensive manner. Ultimately it will benefit the organization a lot. The five basic things that can make a leader more authentic are:

-       Passion and purpose

- Behavior and values
- Connection and Relationships
- Self-disciplined and consistency
- Compassion and heart

In this section, let us have a look at all of these, one by one in brief.

Authentic leaders display a sense of purpose, and they understand what they want. They also understand the path of their mission. Their purpose becomes their passion. Passionate people love what they do. They are inspired to do their job and care for it as well. Showing passion for the job enables a leader to lead by example. Leaders who demonstrate passion, inspire employees to work with passion as well. This leads to a positive work and job atmosphere. Thanks to the passion, people can brainstorm and find new ideas and ways to succeed.

Authentic leaders demonstrate a sense of value. They understand that their behavior should be based on values and that they should not compromise with their ideals, values, and ideas. Changing one's values according to the situation makes you seem fake. People will find you untrustworthy. The customer is the king, which means that your behavior should be customer-oriented. Similarly, as a leader, you should be considerate about the feelings of others, and this should reflect in your values as well. Taking shortcuts and different routes are fine as long as you do not forgo your ideals for it. Bending the rules for your own gains may give you short-term benefits, but in the long term, it will hinder your progress.

Authentic leaders display a sense of connection and bonding. They create and maintain positive bonds and relationships with their friends and colleagues. They are not only willing to share their ideas and experiences, but they are also humble enough to listen to the experiences of their subordinates. They prefer communicating with others as it allows them to understand people. A good leader needs to be open about things, ideas, and the thought processes behind them. He or she should be able to demonstrate respect towards others' ideas. The more you connect with people, the more they will want to connect with you and will respect you as well. Be open to things, and you will more be committed towards ideas and goals.

Self-discipline is another quality that is essential for leaders. It allows leaders to be focused and determined. It allows them to focus on a goal and move forward on the path towards that goal with total dedication and discipline. They do not falter even if they experience setbacks. They are consistent and are calm, cool, and consistent. They handle a difficult and stressful situation with ease and calm. They try to keep away stress, confusion, and similar problems. Their cool and composed attitude allows them and others to stay on track.

The last quality that makes leaders authentic is their compassion and heart. They are sensitive to the needs and requirements of others. They are always willing to help others. When people are stressed, they try to solve their problems. They help individuals understand the dynamics of groups and teams. They help people to burst their stress. They are genuinely concerned about the wellbeing of their employees and followers.

Overall, all these qualities can make you an authentic leader. Your passion, consistency, behavior, compassion, and ability to connect with people can help you become a great leader. It is clear that an authentic leader not only cares about himself or herself but also cares for his or her job and employees. It allows such people to be productive, happy and focused. It is true that leadership can be a stressful process, but it is still necessary to be composed and calm all the time.

Remember, authenticity can make you a great leader.

Dominance

There are two strategies that leaders and professionals all over the world use to either gain or maintain their status. These two strategies are prestige and dominance. Both of these strategies are tried and tested and prominent throughout the world of business and leadership. Dominance consists of coercion, power, and intimidation in team situations. Similarly, prestige involves skills, valuable knowledge, and respect. It is clear from the above differentiation; prestige is a far more positive way of gaining status. However, the world is not divided into black and white, and thus a leader needs to possess both the strategies. A leader needs to use both the strategies and use them according to situations. Navigating the society is already a difficult task, and as a leader, the difficulty and complexity of this task becomes even more intense.

According to research, both strategies are essential and effective at displaying dominance and influencing other people. Dominance is a great way of gaining power, but it rarely begets respect. It often kills the wellbeing of a team or group. It is true that dominant people rarely enjoy love and popularity as compared to their 'prestigious' counterparts; it has been observed that sometimes a dominant or a dominance-oriented leader is necessary. Sometimes dominance is better suited for a task as compared to prestige.

Dominant workers generally display superiority, arrogance, and conceit. They tend to possess manipulative, aggressive, and disagreeable personality that is not appreciated by anyone. They also tend to have a high score on the 'dark triad' of personality. This dark triad consists of three traits viz. Narcissism, Machiavellianism, and psychopathy.

People who use prestige often tend to display pride and humility. People who have prestige are agreeable. They also have a lot of self-esteem. They tend to display social monitoring skills, a need for affiliation, conscientiousness. They are scared of negative results and evaluation.

In teams, members who are dominant tend to look at others as either foes or friends. They try to analyze whether a person is useful in attaining their own goals or not. They are often hungry for power. People who use prestige instead are more focused on sharing their skills and knowledge with others. It is no wonder that prestige-oriented people are more popular than dominant members in groups.

Leaders who prefer dominance over prestige can go to any length to protect their power. They can even destroy their team and team members to safeguard their interests. They can coerce people with the help of punishment and reward both. For them, talented and strong members of the group are often a threat. They would rather eliminate the threat instead of utilizing them for the interests of the team. They would rather work with an incompetent worker instead of promoting a competent and strong worker. Such leaders often try to prevent associations and bonding among their team. Bonding often leads to the formation of alliances. It is easy to break an individual but breaking an alliance takes a lot of time and efforts.

Prestigious leaders promote positive relationship and bonding among their colleagues and team members. For them, the success of the team matters more than their own personal success. They are more likely to sacrifice their power for the greater good, which makes them immensely popular.

Then why would a group want to work under a dominant leader? Prestige, as it is apparent, is a preferable and comfortable strategy of working in a team. Nobody likes a coercive, power-hungry, aggressive, arrogant, and Machiavellian leader. But then, research says that people do desire dominant leaders in certain situations.

Groups tend to prefer dominant leaders only when conflicts arise in their group. They also prefer dominant leaders when an outside party attacks the group. The traits of dominant leaders, such as power-hungriness and aggressiveness, are often useful in such situations. In such situations, the skills and traits of a prestige leader, such as altruism are not appreciated. In fact, they can be looked down upon, and such leaders may be considered weak as well. In the face of conflicts, dominant leaders can change and adjust their tendencies slightly according to the needs of their group. Instead of discarding the strongest player of the team (to discard threat) they may promote them to help their team win.

Narcissism

Narcissistic style of leadership involves leaders that are interested in their interests. They tend to prioritize their ideas and gains often at the cost of other people.

Narcissistic leaders are often hostile, dominant, and arrogant. This style of leadership can often turn destructive, especially when the person is driven by a constant need for approval, power, and admiration. While the negative aspects of narcissistic behavior can ruin one's career, the positive attributes can help you develop good leadership qualities as well.

Let us have a look at some common traits that are associated with narcissistic leaders.

Vision

One of the positive aspects of narcissistic leaders is that they lead with vision. They understand the importance of vision and understand how important it is for people as well. Such leaders are able to see the big picture and rarely 'imagine' things. They often attempt to create things that are not already available.

Admiration

Narcissistic people love being admired and adored. They love having star-struck followers and fans. They possess the gift of attracting followers and often they possess many attractive qualities such as developed articulation and verbal skills. These leaders are often great orators and can deliver extremely moving speeches. They are charismatic and bold.

Criticism

A negative trait associated with these leaders is that they are extremely sensitive. They are especially sensitive to harsh criticism and can barely tolerate it. Unlike other leaders who receive criticism in a constructive way, narcissistic leaders often brood over it. They do not like dissenting opinions and despise slights. They act abrasively towards people who go against them or have a negative opinion about them or their work.

Lack of listening skills

Narcissistic leaders are self-centered, and they rarely pay any attention to others and their ideas. They do not possess good listening skills and open talk about them and their ideas only. This disinterest in listening often results in the formation of a defense mechanism that they use against criticism.

Narcissistic leaders often do not care about their subordinates and their contributions. They do not pay attention to the opinions of others.

Relationships

Healthy narcissistic leaders often show real concern about others. They also respect others' values, ideas, and opinions. Destructive narcissistic leaders, however, do not care for the opinions of others. They will often demean them and their ideas without any sense of guilt or remorse.

Consistency

A leader who possesses healthy levels of narcissism also possesses a set of values that they strictly adhere to. They follow a pre-planned path and rarely go haywire. Destructive narcissistic leaders, in turn, change all the time. They have no values and are known to be fickle. They are also easily bored, as well.

Large projects

Narcissistic leaders dream of building empires (and even taking over the world). They believe that leaving a legacy after them is a must. They often seek endeavors that can help them do this. They often hire subordinates and make plans that will help them reach their dreams. A narcissistic leader will not stop and will continuously create new endeavors and companies.

Empathy

Narcissistic leaders crave understanding and empathy from others; however, they rarely get it. Similarly, they are rarely empathetic towards others as well. Many popular and successful narcissistic leaders are known for their non-empathetic nature. Lack of empathy can prove to be a pro as well as a con. While lack of empathy can help you be practical and strong in the time of chaos, it can also trample upon the feelings of subordinates and employees.

Competitive

As it is clear from above, narcissistic leaders are extremely competitive. They are ruthless and will pursue victory in a bold and relentless manner. They take everything seriously. Even the simplest games can become a matter of life and death for them. A lot of narcissistic leaders do not show remorse and do not care about conscience either. Due to this, they often try to grab victory using licentious ways as well.

Lack of mentoring skills

Many narcissistic leaders lack empathy and are often self-centered; this is why it is almost impossible to find a narcissistic leader who is also a good mentor. Similarly, such leaders cannot be mentored as well. When they do mentor someone, they do not coach people, they just instruct. They cannot tolerate their protégés to become bigger than them.

Don't Use Fear

Fear is a popular workplace tactic, but not many people acknowledge it as it is often hidden. On the surface level, fear is rarely visible, but it often has deep roots in the core of the organization. Fear is not easy to pinpoint but still has a significant influence on the organization. Fear is often generated and spread from people in leadership positions.

The opposite of leading by fear is leading by respect. Both these methods may seem to be similar on a superficial level; however, they are two different methods that lead to vastly different results.

Leading with fear can lead to some short-term benefits. It can lead to immediate action and can also create a sense of urgency and anxiety, which can lead to activity. But such activity rarely leads to a lot of productivity. Leaders do not often use fear to control people; only leaders who are desperate use it as a last resort. This dark side of leading can often lead to a lot of problems. This is why respect-based leadership is often promoted as a healthy alternative to fear-based leadership. Respect-based leadership has enormous benefits and can lead to a lot of positive results. You can begin using this kind of leadership right away, and you will soon start noticing the positive effects.

Let us have a brief look at the key traits of both these leadership styles. This section will allow you to understand the difference between these two and will prove how 'respect' can help you more than 'fear'.

Fear Disempowers

Fear-based leadership creates employees who are self-centered. They only care about themselves and rarely focus on others. People who are motivated by fear rarely look beyond them. They instinctively go into survival mode. They only care about their own jobs. They do not care for the outcome of their organizations and their customers as well. This creates a bad working atmosphere where every employee ultimately becomes narcissistic and self-obsessed. The company's focus changes from profit and customers.

Respect Empowers

Good leaders create good employees. They find methods that allow them to discover best in people. They allow employees to use their full potential. Their energy is desirable. They are inspiring and allow others to go beyond their limits. They do not use coercion to make others work. Inspired leaders create inspired employees and inspired employees to inspire other employees as well. This, in turn, creates an atmosphere of positivity in the company.

Empowered employees' focus externally. They tend to look for out of the box solutions. They like to create a better working atmosphere and like to create better teams as well.

Fear: Lack of creativity and communication

People who lead with fear often create cynical, anxious, and intimidated employees. Such employees rarely trust their leaders and are often toxic to their teams. Fear breeds dishonesty and lack of transparency in the team. Both these factors are essential if you want communication to be successful among your team. If employees are too afraid to bring something up, an aura of dysfunction will settle on the organization. Fear limits rationality. Limited rationality leads to poor decision-making and can truncate action as well.

Fear often leads to concerned and troubled employees. Such employees do not enjoy their jobs, and they are often looking for other options. This behavior rarely leads to successful and innovative ideas. It also creates a stagnant and useless staff. People lose their ability to be creative and innovative. Both these factors are essential if you want to succeed, especially in the modern world. Companies with 'scared' employees can rarely succeed in the competitive world of entrepreneurship. Feat kills imagination and ingenuity. Fear takes away the right of thinking in a free and independent way. If your company uses this method for a long time, your opponents will rise above you.

Respect: Creativity and Communication

Respect is a great way to lead people. Respect always begets respect. Powerful and bold leaders always put their team and team members first. This allows them to win their trust and confidence. The employees who trust their leaders can initiate open communications with them.

Another aspect of respect is becoming a team player. Instead of being 'leader' all the time, you should allow others to voice their opinions, ideas, and feedback as well. You should also ask your team members to pinpoint your weaknesses and allow them to solve them. Be authentic while doing so, or your employees will lose their trust in you. Your team should believe and understand that you are not just and authority figure and that you are a real, approachable human being with whom they can communicate.

Fear Is a Disguise

Leaders often use fear-based leadership because they want to hide their insecurities and fear. Many leaders are aware of this, while many others do it subconsciously. A leader generally uses this method to hide behind a secure wall of intimidation. He or she can appear tough, but on the inside, he or she is broken and scared. This kind of approach soon makes the employees doubt their own skills and creates an overall lack of confidence in the group.

Respect Is Genuine

Leaders who are genuinely respected do not stop until they have achieved their goals. They continue to persevere and are passionate about their work. They hold their employees in high esteem. Great leaders can not only inspire others, but they can also motivate them to do jobs that the employees did not think they could do. They gain respect by leading by example.

Respected leaders are passionate about their group and the purpose behind their group. Their passion is often contagious, and the group members try to emulate this. The members do not care for the title of their leader, even if the title is revoked, the person will still be respected. Even the leaders don't care about the position are driven by their passion for their work.

Fear-based leadership really is not leadership as it is mainly focused on bossing and dominating others. A leader who uses this technique just barks around orders and looks at his employees as commodities that can be expended. They only seek validation and recognition. They use threats to manage people.

Real leaders can inspire and empower people around them with the help of purpose and passion. They guide people by leading by example.

Eliminating Negativity

Negativity is a virus that can lead to a severe infection that ultimately can even destroy and organization. Everyone is highly susceptible to negativity, but people who are uncertain are especially susceptible to it. Uncertainty can make us panic and make rash decisions.

Our brain works continuously on Bayesian inferences. This means it keeps a close eye on the surrounding world and its workings. Your brain observes the world and creates an imaginary model in your head. It uses this model to make predictions about reality. When these predictions clash with the 'real reality', the brain tweaks the model and gets everything running once again. While our brain can handle simple clashes, it cannot tolerate frequent and constant clashes. If it cannot predict what will happen next, you start to panic. Uncertainty thus is the main cause behind panic.

While all kinds of uncertainty lead to panic, 'irreducible uncertainty' is the main culprit. This uncertainty represents the uncertainty in while you cannot do anything about a situation. Uncertainty creates a sort of chain of toxic negativity.

There are many different ways of reducing or minimizing negativity. Let us have a look at a five-step solution for this problem in this section.

Define the way

Before you even begin, it is necessary to remind yourself of what you are supposed to do and how you should do it. You should also keep in mind how and why are you supposed to do the thing. This will enable you to control your employees without making them feel miserable.

Defining the territory

Once you have defined a path, it is now time to define territories as well as the roles of people. All your team members or employees need to know their duties and what is expected of them. This will allow you to keep your employees in control.

Defining your thoughts

A leader should always be open about his or her thoughts, ideas and decisions. He or she should not hide them, or the employees will not find their leader trustworthy. Your employees need to be reassured about your views and ideas frequently. They also need to be reassured about their future in the company.

Defining your cooperation

Be genuine. Nobody likes fake people. It is recommended to listen to your employees, as this will enhance their trust in you.

Define the culture

Instead of focusing on negativity, try to formulate a culture of optimism and positivity. Our surroundings play a major role in deciding our behavior. The more optimistic the atmosphere will be, the more positive you will act.

Chapter Five: Leadership Styles

Leadership is a highly unique and individualistic concept. Its facets and traits change according to individuals, yet it is possible to divide it into certain groups using common characteristics. In this section, let us have a look at some of the most common forms or styles of leadership.

Autocratic or Authoritarian Style

Autocratic style of leadership is also known as the authoritarian leadership style. It is known for its individual control on decisions in which little to no input is desired from the group members. Autocratic leaders generally make choices based on their judgments and ideas. They almost never accept advice from their followers. Autocratic leaders prefer authoritarian and absolute control over their team.

Autocratic leadership style may seem to be a bit erratic, but it has a lot of benefits as well. Often people who use this approach a lot are considered to be dictatorial or bossy, but such behavior can also have a lot of benefits in certain situations. It depends on the user when to use the authoritarian style of leadership. Using it in the wrong situation can lead to a lot of problems as well. Using this type of leadership in an unknown group or situation can be especially harmful.

Characteristics of Autocratic Leadership

Here is a list of some of the primary characteristics of autocratic leadership

- Leaders make all the decisions.
- Almost no input is desired or accepted by the team members.

- Team members are not trusted with important tasks and decisions.
- All processes and methods are dictated by the leader.
- Work is rarely creative.
- Work is often rigid and structured.
- Rules are crucial and are followed with dedication.

Benefits

Here is a list of benefits of the autocratic leadership style.

- This type of leadership provides a lot of oversight and a clear chain of command.
- Leaders make quick decisions, especially in difficult situations.
- Is excellent in situations where strong leadership is required.

As said above the autocratic style of leadership may sound to be negative and useless. It is true that it may lead to negative implications when it is applied to wrong situations or is overused, but it can also lead to a lot of benefits. For instance, when a leader needs to make a quick decision, it is always better to use the autocratic method instead of holding long discussions with the team members. Certain difficult projects may require a strong and autocratic leader for efficiency and success.

If the leader is the most knowledgeable and experienced person in the group, then, it is best to use the autocratic style.

Uses

The autocratic style of leadership can be quite effective in small groups where leadership is absent or negligible. For instance, it can be really beneficial for student groups/ coworkers who are not at all organized. This will not only lead to personal problems but can also cause havoc in the group dynamics. In such situations are strong, and autocratic leader can take charge of the group and change it for good. He or she can help and segregate the tasks. He or she can also help with the deadlines.

Certain group projects work best when a person is assigned to be the leader or if a person himself or herself takes up the role of the leader. This method can help you to assign tasks, set clear goals and roles etc. This way, the group will be able to finish the project on time, and all the members will be able to contribute equally as well.

This style of leadership is also suitable in situations where a lot of pressure is involved. Certain situations like military conflicts are quite stressful and require immediate attention. In such situations, it is necessary to use the autocratic style of leadership. This way, each member of the group will be able to pay close attention to specific tasks and will be able to make complex decisions quickly.

This kind of leadership can also help team members to become highly skilled at performing certain duties. This is great for the health and development of the group.

Another field that can really benefit from the autocratic style of leadership is construction and manufacturing. In this situation, each person needs to have a clearly assigned task, rules, and deadline that they need to follow. An autocratic style of leadership can work wonders in such a situation because it will keep away the accidents and injuries.

Drawbacks

Here is a small list of all the problems associated with autocratic leadership

- The group is not allowed to present its views.
- Is bad for the morale of the team members.

- Can lead to resentment.
- May lead to the death of creativity.

As it is clear from the last section that the autocratic style of leadership can be quite beneficial at times, however, it is still quite problematic and can lead to a lot of problems in many situations.

People who misuse this style are often seen to be controlling, bossy, and dictatorial. This creates resentment and problems among the group members. Group members can feel that they have no say or input in any of the things. This feeling is especially strong in members who are capable and skilled. If they are not allowed to use their pros in a constructive way, their potential remains unused.

Problems

Some of the most common problems associated with autocratic leadership include:

1. It does not encourage group input, as autocratic leaders tend to make decisions without consulting with others. The team members may not appreciate this as they may feel that they cannot contribute their ideas. Autocratic leaders often destroy creativity. This may affect the performance of the team in a negative way.

2. Autocratic leaders often overlook the expertise and knowledge of their group members. They avoid consulting their group members while making decisions that can lead to the failure of the group.

3. Autocracy can also cause problems with the morale of the group. People tend to perform better when they are happy and pleased with their atmosphere. Happiness is often derived when people believe that they are helping their group and are

doing something worthwhile. Autocracy takes away this feeling that makes employees stifled and dissatisfied.

Autocratic Leaders: Survival Guide

As it is clear that the autocratic style of leadership can really work wonders in some situations, but in others, it can cause a lot of problems. It is not an appropriate approach for all situations and groups. If you are an autocratic leader or this happens to be your dominant style, there are certain things that you need to consider to make your style more friendly and open.

Listen

Listen to your group members. This does not mean that you should always follow or use their advice, but listening can still help. Your subordinates will start feeling that they are valuable and hold some importance in the group. If you do not listen to your team members, they will often feel rejected or ignored. Keeping an open mind will make your group more pleasant and productive.

Rules

If you want your team members to follow your rules, you need to establish them firmly in the beginning. You need to ensure all the guidelines are in check and well established. Check whether your team members know that they need to follow the rules.

Knowledge and Tools

Provide your group members with the tools and knowledge that they need. Offer them assistance whenever required. Also, offer them opportunities to get training and take courses.

Reliability

Reliability is the key in any relationship, including leader and employee. If you are not reliable, your team members will quickly lose respect for you. If you expect your group members to follow the rules, you should follow them as well.

Success

Always praise your group members whenever they deserve it. Constant criticism will break their morale.

Autocratic leadership is a strict no-no for many, but you can cherry-pick certain elements from this style to make your own leadership style more potent. You just need to understand the style and use the elements wisely. If you maintain a balance between the democratic and autocratic style, you will be able to lead your group in a better way.

Participative or Democratic Style

Participative style of leadership is also known as the democratic or shared style of leadership. In this style, the group members take an active part in the decision-making processes. This style is versatile and can be used in many different scenarios, including government, businesses, schools etc.

In this style, every member of the group is allowed to participate in the group and exchange their ideas freely. In this method, ideas are allowed to flow freely, and everyone is treated equally. The leader is supposed to offer guidance to the group. He or she is the person who decides the sequence of ideas and what decisions should be made.

According to various studies, democratic leadership is one of the best and effective types of leaderships. It is productive and can allow all the members of the group to participate in important decisions. It can also help the morale of the group.

Characteristics

Here are some of the primary characteristics associated with this kind of leadership:

- Encouragement: In this style, members are encouraged to share their opinions and ideas. (The leader has the final say.)
- Engaging: This style of leadership is far more encouraging and engaging.
- Creativity: In this style, creativity is not only encouraged, but it is also rewarded.

Traits

Following are the traits that are commonly observed in democratic leaders:

- Honesty: Democratic leaders are reliable and honest.
- Intelligence: It takes a lot of intelligence to listen and understand the views of others and then make a wise decision using the views. Democratic leaders are smart and intelligent.
- Courage: Listening to others and using their ideas can lead to a lot of potential problems. Democratic leaders thus need to be courageous.
- Creative: A democratic leader and a democratic group are supposed to be creative.
- Competent: A leader should be competent if he wants to use the democratic style of leadership.
- Fairness: A democratic leader needs to be fair so that he or she can listen to the views and ideas of the group member with patience.

Strong democratic leaders can instill respect and trust in their followers. They are sincere because they often base their decisions on values and morals. They are inspired and love to contribute to the group. Good democratic leaders use diverse opinions and rarely silence dissent. Many democratic leaders prefer dissent over sycophancy.

Benefits

Here is a list of all the benefits associated with a democratic style of leadership:

- Creative solutions and more ideas.
- Group members are committed.
- The group is more productive than other methods.

As group members are encouraged to share their ideas and thoughts in this style of leadership, it often leads to more creative solutions and better ideas. Group members appreciate working in a democratic group because they feel more involved. This way, they care about the end results are thus committed to the projects as well.

Drawbacks

Here is a list of all the drawbacks of the democratic style of leadership:

- Failure related to communication.
- Problems in decision making because of unskilled group members.
- Minority opinions are ignored.

It is true that the democratic style of leadership is considered to be one of the most effective styles of leadership, but it still has some drawbacks. For instance, in situations where the roles are unclear, the democratic style of leadership will almost always fail. In some cases where the group members lack the necessary skills or knowledge, they will not be able to make quality contributions to the group.

Where to Use Democratic Leadership

Democratic leadership can be used in a lot of situations nowadays. It works great in a talented and highly skilled group. It allows people to contribute and is thus great in schools as well.

Laissez-faire or Free-rein

Laissez-faire leadership is also known as a delegative style of leadership. It is a hands-off style of leadership in which the group members are allowed to make the decisions. According to researchers, this style of leadership is the least productive of all other styles of leadership.

While it is known to be less productive, it still has some positive aspects. There exist certain settings where this kind of leadership can work wonders.

Traits of Laissez-faire Leadership

This type of leadership is well known for the following things:

● Guidance: In this style of leadership employees do not receive guidance from their employers.
● Freedom: This method provides total freedom to the group members.
● Provisions: The leaders of these groups only provide the necessary resources and tools to the members.
● Solutions: The group members are expected to use the above resources. The employees are supposed to use their experience the provided resources to tackle the problems.

● Power: Members of these groups are handed over power by the leaders, but the leaders are still expected to take responsibility for the group and the decisions made.

There have been many famous politicians, entrepreneurs, and great leaders who have used certain elements from this method. For instance, Steve Jobs used to give his team members some directions while the members were supposed to come up with ideas and solutions themselves. Similarly, former President Herbert Hoover was well known for his 'relaxed' approach towards governing.

Benefits

Like all the other styles of leadership, this method too has many benefits as well as drawbacks.

1. The Laissez-faire style is particularly effective if it is used correctly in the right situations and with the right groups.
2. This method is especially suitable for people who possess skills and creativity. If the group members are motivated, skilled, and capable of independent work, then a Laissez-faire leader will help them achieve success. Such groups require little to no advice and guidance and are thus self-sufficient.
3. This method is also suitable for groups where the members are more skilled than the leader. As the team members are experts of the area, the Laissez-faire style can allow them to illustrate their knowledge about the topic and skills related to the subject.
4. In situations where independence is valuable, this method of leadership can work really well. The autonomy of this leadership style allows people to be more satisfied with their job. This style of leadership is especially great for groups where the group members are motivated and passionate about their jobs.

5. The leaders who follow this style are often available for feedback and consultation. These leaders can provide insight and guidance at the beginning of the project and then allow the group members to do their job on their own.

6. This kind of leadership needs a lot of trusts. Leaders should feel confident about the skills and achievements of their group members. They need to be aware of their knowledge, as well.

Negative Aspects of the Laissez-faire style:

This style of leadership is not recommended for situations where the group members do not possess the necessary skills, experience, and knowledge to make decisions. This style is notorious for producing bad performance, bad results, and low group satisfaction.

Not everyone is great at setting their own deadlines and managing their own projects. People often find solving their own problems difficult as well. In such situations, the project may soon go off-track, and the group may miss crucial deadlines.

No role awareness

The Laissez-faire style of leadership can lead to a lot of problems in some situations because, in this style, the roles are not defined within the group. Team members receive little to no guidance and are often unaware of the things that they are supposed to do.

Lack of involvement

The leaders who follow this style of leadership are often withdrawn and uninvolved. This can lead to confusion. The group members may think that the leader does not care about what is happening in the group. This makes the members unconcerned as well.

Low accountability

It is easy to abuse this method of leadership. Leaders may use it to avoid personal responsibilities. If the goals are not achieved, the leader can simply blame the team members and accuse them of not finishing their tasks.

Passivity and avoidance

This style of leadership can lead to lethargy and passivity. People can even avoid leadership altogether. Such leaders will avoid doing anything to motivate their group members and will make no attempt to involve them in-group decisions.

If the group members are unskilled and are unfamiliar with the task of the process, it is recommended to use a more hands-on approach. With time the group members will gain more expertise, and the leader can then switch back to a more laid-back style of leadership that will allow the group members more freedom and independence.

Where to Use Laissez-faire Approach

If you are a Laissez-faire leader, then there are some situations and areas where you can do wonders. This method is well suited for a creative field where people are highly motivated, creative, and skilled. This method can lead to great results in such fields.

For instance, a delegative leader will work great in product design and related fields. In such fields, all the team members are highly creative and well trained. They require little to no management (or assistance). An effective Laissez-faire leader will just provide minimal guidance and oversight to the team members, and the team will still produce great results.

Laissez-faire leaders are generally great at providing the initial data and background to begin a project. This information is great for teams that are self-managed. By providing the team members all the information and tools that they need at the beginning of the assignment, the team will understand what they are supposed to do and will figure out how to do it.

While the Laissez-faire method is great in such groups, it is still recommended to use different leadership methods in different phases of the assignment. For instance, this method can be used in the initial stage of the task, i.e. in the brainstorming session. Later it is recommended to use a more insightful and 'directive' style of leadership.

This style may prove to be difficult in situations where a lot of precision, oversight, and attention is required. In situations where every detail needs to be perfect and timely, this method will fail. In such situations, it is better to use a more managerial or authoritarian style instead. Utilizing the Laissez-faire method in this scenario can lead to a lot of problems, including poor performance, missed deadlines, and lack of direction. This is especially true if the group is unskilled.

It is true that the Laissez-faire method is usually considered to be a style of leadership that can have can negative implications. Yet it can prove to be highly beneficial in many different situations. It is especially useful in groups where all the members are equally skilled and motivated. In such groups, this method can lead to the best results possible. Team members are allowed to use their freedom and are not micromanaged like all the time, so they feel more creative and inspired.

If you are this kind of leader, try to think of situations where you can use this method freely. In groups where more insight is needed, it is recommended to pair this method with some other form of leadership, such as the democratic or the authoritarian method. By examining your own style of leadership, you can become a great leader.

Task-oriented and relationship-oriented

As explained above, leadership varies a lot from person to person. It is subject to the individual's attitude, their surroundings, the atmosphere, etc. It also depends on how they implement plans, how they provide direction, and how they motivate people. In every business endeavor, the style of leadership changes and fluctuates significantly.

Around 83% of organizations believe that it is necessary to develop leaders at all levels. Around 43% of organizations have made it their top priority to bridge the gap between all leader levels. More and more money is being spent on the development of leadership as compared to any other area. Still, around 71% of organizations do not believe that their leaders can lead their organization into the future. If you want to make the best decisions in your training, then it is necessary to know which style of leadership you currently possess and how you can adjust it to enhance the overall performance of your organization.

The two most commonly used and seen styles of leadership are task-oriented leadership and people-oriented leadership. People-oriented leadership is also known as a relationship-oriented leadership style. These two have been a hotly debated topic since forever. Each style has its own pros and cons. In this section, let us have a look at the pros and cons of both the methods.

Task-Oriented Leadership Advantages and Disadvantages

Pros

There are several characteristics and traits that make task-oriented leaders the best leaders around. These leaders are highly proficient and can get things done on time. These leaders create easy to understand and follow methods and instructions due to which their group finishes work on time. This style of leadership is great if you want to maintain high standards of optimal efficiency. Employees who desire structure and do not well on their own can really benefit from this kind of leadership, as it is task-oriented, organized, and structured. It is also deadline-driven, which makes it efficient.

Cons

Some of the most common cons of this style of leadership include lack of autonomy and independence for employees. Employees are not allowed to show their creativity in this method. This can lead to dropping in the morale of the group. When an employee is forced to work in a strict atmosphere with strict deadlines, the company culture goes down significantly. Many employees can become rebellious in such situations, especially if they are skilled and self-motivated.

Another negative aspect of this kind of leadership style is that it hinders creative thinking. It can cause a negative effect on the company's products and its image. It kills innovation and is thus not recommended for companies that are closely related to arts.

Focus

1.   Finishing Jobs: This style of leadership is thoroughly focused on finishing the project at hand as soon as possible.

2. Effective goal setting: For this method to work, the leader sets the goal and formulates a path to reach the goal in the initial stages. This keeps the team focused.

3. Schedules: This method is highly focused on deadlines and keeping schedules.

4. Goals: As said earlier, this method is extremely goal-oriented and strives hard to produce the desired results.

People-Oriented Leadership Advantages and Disadvantages

Pros

People-oriented style of leadership is the best for employees as they enjoy the central place in this style. This style tries to appreciate the workers for the work they do. It focuses heavily on employee and employer relationship. This makes the employees think that they are a crucial part of the company, which in turn makes them passionate and motivated. They believe that they can help the company and the group become a great success if they put in efforts.

Cons

This style of leadership comes with many different challenges. It is possible that the employees may end up feeling burdened with responsibilities. They may feel overwhelmed and confused. Some employees cannot work without directions, and such employees will struggle a lot under a people-oriented leader. Many ineffective decisions can be made due to inconsistent skills of the team members. The business may suffer a lot of certain aspects of finance are neglected.

Focus

1.   Workers: In this style of leadership, the satisfaction and wellbeing of the workers are considered to be the most important aspect. This method is concerned with the workers and their mental and physical health and whether they are feeling motivated or not.

2.   Interaction: This method focuses on conversation and connection between colleagues. It facilitates positive interaction between colleagues, which can produce productive results.

3.   Team building: To facilitate interaction between colleagues, this method focuses on team-building exercises and conducts various meetings frequently.

Thus, it is clear that you cannot be task-oriented as well as people-oriented at the same time. You need to decide which path to choose else you will end up being a confused and failed leader. The best way to be a great leader is by picking up the best parts from each style of management and leadership. This will help you to make a combination of various skills and styles that will allow you to cultivate a great persona and working atmosphere as well. Different situations need different approaches. If you keep the pros and cons of all the styles in mind, you can always find the best-suited approach for a situation. Ultimately you will be able to develop a style of leadership that will be unique, personal, and well cultivated and calculated.

Paternalism

Paternalism or paternalistic leadership is a type of leadership style that consists of a dominant authoritative personality who often acts as a patriarch or a matriarch and treats his or her employees as members of a large family. In turn, the employees trust and obey the leader and are loyal towards him or her.

This type of leadership style creates and amicable atmosphere at the workplace in which the employees consider the leader and other employees as their family. Everyone wants to be a part of a family; it is just our natural human tendency. Like families, we have heads in organizations who hold an authoritative position. These leaders decide what is best for the team and make decisions accordingly. This is why in this method it is necessary for the leader to be caring and optimistic.

Elements of Paternalistic Leadership

This kind of leadership is highly common in Asian nations. In fact, it is believed that this style originated in China. This style of leadership consists of three main elements, they are:

- Autocratic leadership
- Benevolent leadership
- Moral leadership

Let us have a look at them one by one.

Autocratic Leadership

The historical as well as the philosophical background of this kind of leadership can be traced back to Confucianism in China. In this style, every leader possesses the legal right to make decisions and the employees must follow it. The employees are bound to obey their superiors. Leaders of this style tend to monitor their workers closely. They always have the last say in things.

Benevolent Leadership

This too finds references in the ancient Chinese texts. In this style the leader is focused on the familial as well as personal wellbeing of the followers. This is done in a holistic and individualistic style. This the most preferred style of leadership as compared to the other two.

Moral Leadership

In this style, the moral character of the leader and his or her potential is used as a role model by his or her followers. Moral leaders show a lot of respect, kindness, and optimism. They treat people in a non-abusive and fair manner. The main goal of this style of leadership is to serve. Rather than showcasing what they can do, the leaders try to develop the capabilities of their colleagues.

Core Characteristics of Paternalistic Leadership

Paternalistic style of leadership has many traits. Let us have a look at them one by one.

Compassion

A leader cannot be paternalistic if he or she is not compassionate. This element is essential as it enhances the loyalty of the employees towards the organization. Employees are important in a paternalistic style of leadership, and it is the duty of the leader to make the employees feel comfortable and valuable. A leader cannot make his or her followers feel, so unless he or she possess empathy and compassion.

Compassion is innate, but it can also be learned. Compassion meditation is a great way to learn compassion in an altruistic and easy way. If you include compassion mediation in your daily schedule, you will start feeling compassionate for people soon. It will allow you to connect to the feelings of the people, and it will also show how trustworthy you are.

Good Organizational Skills

A paternalistic leader needs to have good organizational skills. They should be able to set their priorities straight while making decisions. Without good organizational skills, their group will not be able to achieve success.

Decisiveness

In this style of leadership, the power to make decisions is completely vested with the leader. Due to this, the leader needs to have a lot of potential, knowledge, and expertise, to make correct decisions. If you follow this style, you cannot contemplate (or make regretful) decisions, as it will hinder the progress of the group.

Making decisions and moving forward is not an easy task, as it requires a lot of thinking and judgment. Remember, with great power comes even greater responsibility.

Empowerment

This style of leadership is highly focused on bringing the best out of the employees. As a leader who follows this style of leadership, you want your employees to grow and develop, just like a parent. Similarly, you want to see your employees succeed and achieve their goals. You also want them to grow as an individual and grow professionally as well.

Empowerment needs a careful balance between micromanagement and autonomy. This kind of leadership does not give the employees a lot of authority, and the leader is supposed to make decisions. The leader, however, does not question the actions of the group members.

Influence

In this style of leadership, it is necessary for the leaders to influence the subordinates. This style provides the leader with a lot of power. While it is strictly not an authoritative style of leadership, the leader still possesses the power to make decisions and change them as well.

There are many different ways in which you can influence people. You can influence people with your knowledge and communication skills. You can also influence them with your wit and charm.

Limitations of Paternalistic Leadership

Let us have a look at some of the limitations of this type of leadership:

1.   Morale: This style can lead to dropping in the morale of the employees, as they are not allowed in the decision-making process.
2.   Dependency: The group members in this style are dependent on the leader as it is the leader who makes all the decisions.
3.   Inclination: It is possible that the subordinates may feel less inclined to find solutions because they will feel less involved.
4.   Irrational Outcome: It is possible that some group members will not be satisfied with the decision of their leader but will still have to follow it.
5.   Struggle: In this style, barring the leader, no other roles are defined properly. Due to this, a lot of internal struggles and issues may arise and disturb the modicum of the group.

Examples

Let us have a look at the paternalistic style of leadership being used in real life:

Executive Leadership

In this style, the employees are considered to be important, and their needs are valued over others. The firm can go to great lengths to avoid layoffs even if the business is losing money. It believes that employees are critical to the health of the firm.

Governments

A government that follows this style of leadership will often try to make quality goods free of cost. It will also try to bring down the costs of products by providing subsidies. These governments often levy heavy duties and taxes on 'harmful' substances, including tobacco, alcohol, etc. This kind of government is associated with regulations, rules, and it tries to control every aspect of the lives of its subjects.

Management

A manager who follows the paternalistic style of leadership will try to boost and develop his or her employees by providing them with opportunities where they can grow. He or she will try to provide them with opportunities that suit their talents and interests. This way, the manager can create a loyal and powerful workforce.

It is thus clear that the paternalistic leadership can be closely related to patriarchy. This is a form of authoritarian style of leadership. This style of leadership is well respected in eastern nations such as China and India. In this style, the point of focus is the big community where the leader is responsible for all his (or her) group members. As said above if the leader creates an environment of loyalty through his or her behavior, this style can work wonders with the employees.

It is assumed that the leader in this style will always make the right decisions. It expects little to nothing from the employees. It does not provide the employees with tools to grow. Thus, this style of leadership can hinder creativity and ultimately, the growth of the organization as well. Some people can think of it as an oppressive form of leadership.

Chapter Six: Leadership Behaviors and Development of Leadership Style and Skills

Character Strengths

Big Five personality factors

The Big Five Traits or the Five Factors is a personality model. It is one of the most popular and highly accepted models in the scientific world. It is not as popular as the Myers-Briggs model in laymen, but it is considered to be more serious and scientifically sound as compared to other models. It studies and analyzes different personalities and their behavior.

This model is known as the Big Five Model because according to this theory all human personalities can be divided into five, distinct and significant sections. These sections are known as dimensions. All of these sections are varied, distinct, unique, and independent of each other. This model is sometimes also known as the OCEAN model or the CANOE model as well. As the name suggests, these are the acronyms for the five dimensions.

According to this model of study, all people can be analyzed using some key factors present in their personality. These factors are responsible for our thoughts as well as behavior. However, personality traits cannot correctly understand a person's behavior in any given situation. The Big Five model then can help people to understand why people act in a certain way in certain situations. Thus, it is not a predictive method. It is not a typical model like other personality models such as the Type A/B personality model or the Myers and Briggs' model. The Big Five model is a 'traits' model.

Type models like the Myers and Briggs' are easy to remember and understand, but they are never scientifically sound. It is impossible to categorize people into simple and easy categories. The Big Five does not sort people into categories. It tries to differentiate people on the basis of their personalities and the traits that they display. Once this is done, the model puts people on a spectrum. A spectrum is far more flexible than regular categories.

It is now time to have a brief look at all the five dimensions as seen in the Big Five Model.

Openness

Openness is often thought to be a tendency to be open about feelings and thoughts. While this is true, in the Big Five Model, openness refers to the ability to take on new experiences, changes, plans, and ideas. Once upon a time this trait was also known as 'intellect', but to avoid unnecessary confusion it is now known as openness and 'intellect' has become obsolete.

A person who possess this trait can think in an abstract way. People who tend to have this trait are often creative, adventurous, and intellectual. These people love playing with ideas and thoughts. They are creative and try to seek new experiences. People who do not show this trait are often more focused, traditional, and practical. They avoid the unknown and off-beat paths. They try to stick to the traditions as much as possible.

Openness as a trait is related to the interconnections present in the regions of the brain. People who have Openness as their dominant trait tend to have more connections as compared to other people.

Conscientiousness

A person who is goal-oriented, persistent, and dedicated is supposed to have a dominant conscientiousness trait. People who have this trait as their dominant trait are often organized and determined. They concentrate on long-term goals and benefits and do not care about short term gratification. People who do not have this trait are often impulsive. They get sidetracked easily.

This trait is closely associated with the frontal lobe activity in the brain. The frontal lobe is considered as the 'executive' area of the brain as it controls, moderates, and regulates 'animal' and instinctual impulses. People who have this trait as their dominant trait tend to use the frontal part of their brain more than other people.

Extraversion

A person who loves the outside world and gets stimulation from it is supposed to have the 'Extraversion' trait. People with this trait try to seek attention from other people. They often like activities and situations where they can make new friends. They desire status, power, administration, and excitement. They are also highly romantically inclined. Compared to them, introverts try to save their energy. They do not care for social rewards.

Extraversion is related to dopamine. Dopamine a neurotransmitter that acts like a reward which keeps us motivated. People who have extraversion as their dominant trait tend to have a lot of dopamine.

Agreeableness

The people who tend to prioritize the needs and desires of other people over their own desires and requirements are said to display the 'agreeable' trait. People who are predominantly agreeable tend to be empathetic as well. They enjoy helping others and making them happy. People who do not display this trait often do not possess empathy. They are selfish and always put their problems in front of problems of others.

If this trait is dominant, then a lot of enhanced activity is seen in the superior temporal gyrus. This area of the brain is related to recognition of emotions and language processing.

Neuroticism

Some people tend to react negatively towards stimulants. They tend to show negative emotions such as guilt, sadness, fear, anxiety, and shame towards stimulants. These reactions can be classified as neuroticism.

This trait is often considered to be a warning sign. The people who tend to show these traits often think that there is something messed up with this world. Fear is supposed to be a reaction to danger, while guilt is a reaction to having done something wrong. But not all people have the same reaction in a moment. People who score a high on this level generally react to things in a negative manner. People who score a low score on this section tend to brush things off and move forward.

In the brain, neuroticism is related to many regions, including the regions that are responsible for processing negative stimuli, including aggressive dogs, angry faces, etc. It is also closely related to the regions that deal with negative emotions. According to a study, high neuroticism can also change the serotonin processing mechanism in the brain.

Big Five Traits and Personality

People are normally described as having low, high, or average levels of all the five traits Each of these factors is independent of other so it is possible that somebody can be highly extroverted by still low in If you want to understand an individual properly using the Big Five Model, it is first necessary to understand how they fair in each of the five dimensions. You can use a Big Five personality test (easily available online) to get a general understanding of your Big Five Traits.

History of the Big Five

The roots of the Big Five model can be traced back to a theory known as the lexical hypothesis. This theory believes that it is possible to create a taxonomy of individual difference by analyzing the language used by us to describe each other. Early researchers used various terms to describe personality traits, including "helpful," "friendly, "aggressive," and "creative." These researchers tried to organize these traits into various groups. For instance, people who were described as being friendly were also described as talkative, gregarious, and outgoing. Researchers soon realized that these trait adjectives often corresponded to the Big Five traits.

Nowadays, the Big Five model forms the basis of modern personality research. It is used to illustrate everything right from our personality, our personality factors, its relation with our income, etc.

Emotional Intelligence

Emotion is a wide range of behaviors, changes in the state of body and mind, and expressed feelings. Feelings, our likes, dislikes, and emotions all provide our lives meaning. They also cause us to be satisfied, happy, dissatisfied, or sad. Intelligence can be defined as the ability to use and gain knowledge and skills. If both of these are combined, we get Emotional Intelligence that can be defined as our ability to deal with other people efficiently. By understanding our own feelings, we can understand the feelings of others and evaluate them as well. There are five major elements of emotional intelligence. Let us have a look at them one by one.

Self-Awareness

This can be defined as our ability to recognize and analyze the motivations, moods, and abilities of ourselves. It also includes understanding the effects of the above three on others. If a person wants to become completely self-aware, he or she needs to learn how to monitor his or her emotional state. He or she should be able to identify his or her emotions, as well. Traits that make use emotionally mature include the ability to laugh at oneself, confidence, awareness, and perception.

Self-Regulation

This refers to the ability to control one's emotions and impulses. A good leader should think before he or she speaks or reacts. It is also related to the ability to express oneself in an appropriate manner.

If a person is emotionally mature in this category, he or she will always take responsibility for their action. He or she will be ready to adapt to changes and will always know how to respond appropriately to other people's emotions or irrational behavior.

Motivation

Motivation is closely related to a person's interest in self-improvement and learning. A person who is motivated will often be interested in learning things. A motivated person possesses the strength to keep on going forward even in the face of obstacles. Motivated people not only set goals, but they follow them. A person who is emotionally mature in this skill will have traits such as commitment and initiative. He or she will be committed towards the task and will tend to persevere even in the face of adversity.

Empathy

Empathy refers to the ability to understand other people's reactions and emotions. A person who is self-aware is often always empathetic. If you cannot understand yourself, you will rarely understand others. A person who is emotionally mature in this section will be interested in the problems of other people. He or she will have great anticipatory skills, especially in regard to people and their emotional responses towards situations. They also understand the social norms and the logic behind people's behavior.

Social Skills

This refers to the ability to pick up on sarcasm, jokes, puns, etc. It is also related to maintaining and managing friendship, friendly customer service, and finding common ground with others. If a person has emotional maturity in this skill, he or she will have good time management skills, good communication skills, and good leadership skills as well. He or she will be able to solve problems with ease and will be able to manage a large group of people effortlessly. He or she will possess excellent persuasion and negotiation skills.

Emotional intelligence plays a significant role in maintaining positive relationships with the people around them. This allows leaders to become successful leaders. Successful leaders are well known to be emotionally intelligent. They often have great relationships with the people they work with. Nowadays, organizations too tend to pick individuals for leadership positions who are in touch with their emotional side.

Leadership and Intelligence

Management experts have spent a lot of resources to find the connection between intelligence and leadership. That leadership and intelligence are compatible and correlated is a well-known fact.

The Connection between Leadership and Intelligence

Intelligent Leaders Listen and Learn

If you want to become a successful leader, you need to possess the qualities of listening to others and taking inputs from them. You should be able to listen and take inputs from everyone, including your subordinates as well. Intelligent leaders do not only care about plans but also know how to utilize others and get their help to plan activities. Leadership is a group activity and if you ever feel that your leadership is getting dangerously close to dictatorship, abort it.

Intelligence is essential as it allows leaders to evaluate other peoples' opinions and place them into the plans hypothetically. This way, leaders can check whether an idea can work in the plan or not. A great leader will always try to get valuable inputs from employees. This will not only help his or her plan, but it will also boost the confidence and morale of his or her employees.

A great leader understands the importance of communication. He or she should be able to communicate with his or her employees. Leaders need to talk and discuss their ideas with their employees. Employees can teach leaders a lot. Leaders need to adopt new strategies frequently. They can gain these strategies from their employees and team members.

Intelligent Leaders Plan Ahead

One of the major duties of leaders is planning and strategizing in the initial phases. A good leader will know how to adjust his or her plan according to situations and the obstacles. Damage control is essential for all organizations, but if the leader can anticipate impending problems, the damage can be prevented. Intelligent leaders are honest, and they will always let their team members know if there is something wrong or if things are not going according to the plan. Rumors spread quickly in difficult situations, and leaders should always be ready to comfort employees and help the situation to cool down.

Intelligent Leaders and Alliances

A team consists of many different people with varied personalities. Many times, not all team members like each other or are compatible with each other. They may have contrasting ideas or contradicting philosophies. This can lead to disastrous situations if not handled properly. A good leader can solve such problems and create strong bonds and firm alliances. Making different people work for the same goal while collaborating with each other is a sign of an intelligent and successful leader.

An intelligent leader can let his or her team members know how a goal can lead to mutual benefit and convince all the different individuals to work together. Team building and management are two essential skills that all leaders must possess.

Intelligent Leaders Respect

Only getting an MBA cannot help you become a top leader. You need to understand a lot of things and need to have a significant amount of people skills as well. Many top B-school graduates are smart, and this smartness sometimes instils a sense of superiority in them. They can be often boisterous and prideful.

This often leads to problems. Experienced leaders are often stronger than smart but new leaders. It is thus necessary to respect the experience and learn as much as possible from them.

Intelligent Leaders Motivate

Intelligent leaders are often great leaders because they just do not get work done efficiently, but they also motivate their team members all the time. Motivation at the workplace is crucial, and a leader who can motivate team members is always a successful leader.

A leader should be able to understand the needs of his or her team members. He or she should also be able to understand what steps are necessary to motivate people. Each employee is a distinct individual with a distinct set of principles, values, and understandings. A leader cannot use the same method of motivation for each employee. He or she needs to analyze the employee and adjust the motivational method accordingly. Motivating the employees is essential, as they will keep the group alive and thriving.

These are some of the important connections between leadership and intelligence. It is clear from the above section that if a leader wants to be successful, he or she should possess various kinds of intelligence. A smart leader will always be a successful leader.

Self-efficacy for leadership

Efficacy is related to effectiveness and ability. It means the ability to produce the desired result. Thus, self-efficacy means a person's ability in any given situation. Self-efficacy is more about your own belief in your abilities than the true limit. What you believe about yourself has a significant impact on your psychology. It can control the way your brain engages with obstacles and stress.

Another plus point of self-efficacy is that people who have high amounts of it can achieve the given goals by performing the required tasks with ease. They are more likely to accomplish a goal as compared to other people. They are also more intuitive as compared to other people. Self-efficacy can help you avoid being a quitter. It can help you to be successful and bold.

Self-efficacy and Leadership

Nobody likes quitting, as it does not feel good at all. When we quit, we are usually left with insecurities, regret, and pain. We feel as if we have let ourselves down. These are some of the things that no one wants to feel ever. But self-efficacy can help you avoid these. As said earlier, your belief in yourself can help you become successful. So, if you want to become a great leader, you need to trust yourself and believe that you can lead people successfully. Possessing high self-efficacy can help you become a great leader. It affects your performance positively. It can also affect the performance of your group positively as well. Thus, self-efficacy can work wonders for leaders who want to be successful. You may be surprised to know, but as leaders, your perseverance, motivation, thoughts, vulnerabilities, wellbeing, and choices, all are dependent on your self-efficacy. Thus, almost every part of the leadership experience is closely controlled by self-efficacy.

People who have high self-efficacy tend to work better with challenges and problems. If they ever experience a pushback, they can encounter it with calmness. They possess immense self-control and can act with a lot of precision in stressful and difficult situations. They are often willing to put in a lot of efforts to lead the group. They take care of the group's needs.

Leadership Self-Efficacy for Direction Setting

A leader is supposed to plan and guide his or her team towards the goal. If a leader does not possess good directional and guidance skills, he or she can never be a great leader. Self-efficacy can help you become a great director or guide, as it will enable you to be confident about your ability to guide. It will encourage you all the time. It will also boost your confidence regarding problem-solving and other related objectives. Your self-beliefs in this area are often related to your past successes or even failures. They are also closely associated with your beliefs about your intelligence.

Leadership Self-Efficacy for Overcoming Obstacles

One of the major jobs that a leader is supposed to do is overcoming obstacles. The world is constantly changing, and if a leader wants to move with the world, he or she needs to move quickly. A leader needs to learn how to overcome limitations. These limitations can be varied in nature. For instance, a leader may have to face personal limitations, social limitations, individual limitations, etc. A leader needs to possess specific skills to overcome obstacles without harming his or her team. Some skills that are necessary to overcome obstacles include serving others, the ability to pivot, overseeing work, and building momentum. Some other things that are necessary to be a successful taskmaster include drive, self-control, and being action-oriented. A person who is self-motivated and is flexible will always be a great problem solver.

Leadership Self-Efficacy for Gaining Commitment

Achieving commitment is crucial for leadership. You need to have the support of your team if you want to succeed. If no one is committed to your cause, you will not have a team and thus have no one to lead. Gaining commitment comes naturally to some, but for others, it can be incredibly difficult. This is because commitment relies heavily on interpersonal skills. If you possess excellent interpersonal skills, you can easily get others to commit to your cause, but if you lack these skills, it will be quite a task to talk and convince other people. Interpersonal skills are not related to communication skills only; they are also related to your social skills. If you can relate to others with ease and can guide them as well, then you possess decent to good interpersonal skills. Your trustworthiness and clarity of conversation can also make you a great communicator.

All of the above-mentioned skills can be developed with practice and dedication. Treat each conversation or interaction as a practice ground to practice these skills. Soon you will be able to notice a difference in your skills. It is necessary to become a people-person if you want to succeed in the modern world.

Self-awareness for your insecurities is a great way to work through them. It is necessary to reflect upon your ideas and thoughts and insecurities. This will allow you to tackle them effectively. Tackling insecurities is difficult, and it needs a lot of dedication and passion. It is impossible to do it without a lot of self-efficacy.

Thus, it is clear that self-efficacy is necessary for almost all aspects of leadership, and it can really help you become a great leader.

Self-monitoring

Self-monitoring as a concept was first explained by Mark Snyder in 1970s. It is used to analyze how people monitor themselves and how they monitor their behaviors, expressions, self-presentations, and non-verbal communication as well. Each individual has a different capacity of expression and showing their emotions. Some people are great at controlling their emotions and expressions, while some like to wear their mind on their sleeve. Self-monitoring is a personality trait that is useful for regulating your behavior according to the social setting.

People who are concerned with their expression in self-presentation often tend to monitor their audience. Self-monitors try to understand how groups and individuals will react to them. They also pay close attention to how the group or the individual will perceive them. Some personality types act spontaneously, while others tend to control their emotions and expressions purposefully. These people adjust their behavior according to the social situation.

Snyder's self-monitoring scale came into existence in the year 1974. It is used to measure whether an individual has the ability to change their image using impression management in different social interactions and settings. The score is calculated after a small quiz of 25 questions. The test taker is asked to answer the questions according to his or her ideas and thought process. It is used to determine how an individual may use non-verbal signs. It is also used to understand how a particular individual may react in particular situations. The questions are generally True or False type questions.

Low self-monitors

Low self-monitors generally display expressive controls that are concrete. They rarely change their ideas, beliefs, attitudes, and tend to maintain the same disposition in every situation. They never change, regardless of social circumstance. These people often do not care about social context and situations. They believe that displaying an image that is not congruent with their inner-self is fake and should not be done. People who self-monitor often adjust their behavior according to the situation but people who refuse to adjust themselves are often uncompromising, angry, aggressive, and insistent. This is why they are often condemned and disliked. This often leads to the generation of feelings such as isolation, anxiety, anger, guilt, depression, and low self-esteem.

These people are often indiscreet, which makes social situations awkward and uncomfortable. It can often lead to the loss of clients, friends, family, colleague, and in some cases, a career as well. People who are willing to adjust their behavior often find situations easy. People find self-monitors pleasant, receptive, and benevolent.

High self-monitors

People who monitor themselves closely are often known as high self-monitors. They often act in certain ways. They are often highly responsive to situational context and social cues. High self-monitors are often thought of as social pragmatists who can build images to impress others and gain positive feedback. Compared to low self-monitors, high self-monitors often display more expressive control. They are also concerned about the appropriateness of the situation. These people are always ready to adjust their behavior for their own benefits. They are often thought to be pleasant, more receptive, and benevolent, and people react to them in a positive manner as well.

Barriers

Leadership differences affected by gender

A lot of research has been done whether sex differences in leadership exists or not. Similarly, a lot of research has been conducted on whether the differences exist, and whether they exist on relationship levels or task-based levels. Leadership is an intricate process in which individuals guides his or her group towards a goal. According to certain studies, it was found that there exists some sort of difference between the leadership style and methodology of the genders. For instance, women use a more participative style of leadership as compared to men. But there are also certain studies that say that there exists no difference between the genders.

Until recently, almost all leadership positions were held by men and thus men were considered to be more effective leaders. Women rarely got the chance to be leaders leading major corporations and groups, and thus the data regarding their behavior was lacking. But the trend is changing now, and women have become prevalent in the corporate world, enjoying topmost positions as well. Thus, the gender gap is reducing, and the stereotypes associated with leadership are changing as well. But then there are strong proofs that say that the gender gap still exists.

For instance, while women display a lot of effective leadership qualities in some studies, men are still stereotypically considered to be better leaders than women.

There exist a lot of stereotypes regarding the differences between female and male leaders, along with a variety of research and personal anecdotes as well. While there exists a lot of correlation between the accounts and observations, it also reveals a lot of biases. It is possible that these stereotypes are subjective and are perhaps clouded by preconceived notions.

According to preconceived notions and stereotypes, male managers follow a top-down style of leadership. They are also supposed to be hierarchical. On the other hand, female leaders are more egalitarian. They are more supportive and helpful as well. But these are gross stereotypes and generalities. They cannot portray the cultural and individual differences.

Difference Between Male Leader and Female Leaders

Collaboration and Individualism

As per research, female leaders tend to appreciate groups and team efforts more than other leaders. They are more collaborative and try to combine the skills and knowledge of all the team members. Male leaders are supposed to be more individualistic. They create a work atmosphere where people compete with each other because they believe that competition leads to growth.

Egalitarianism and hierarchy

Female bosses praise people for their achievements. Under female bosses' voices are heard and they are valued too. Male bosses focus more on experience, skills, and knowledge. The 'female' approach works great for the morale of the employees while the 'male' approach can help you achieve more predictable results.

Transformational Work and Transactional Work

Female leaders, as said earlier are supposed to be more helpful and supportive. They try to build and develop the skills of their employees and groom them to take up more responsibilities. On the other hand, male bosses use the transactional method of leadership. In this method a person a rewarded whenever they complete a task successfully. Female leaders show a more transformational form of leadership which is good for employees as it leads to continuous learning. The transactional, method, however, is great if you want to get things done quickly.

Perception vs Reality

Women leaders are often described as more compassionate, and this compassion is considered to be a positive trait in female leadership. 'Analytical' is often used to describe a male leadership style. Both analytical and compassionate are subjective terms, and thus, their meanings can differ significantly. It is better to look at leadership styles in a more objective way.

Individual vs. General Traits

Leadership is a subjective term, and it is highly individualistic as well. There is a lot of difference between the leadership styles of individuals. Similarly, there exist a lot of differences between the leadership styles of some men and women. For instance, some men may display stereotypically female leadership traits such as collaboration and compassion, while women may display male traits such as authoritarianism and competitive.

It can be said that a large number of women leaders display a leadership style that is stereotypically associated with men as the hierarchical aspects of the workforce all genders to indulge into specific practices that help them to reach the top.

Non-western

Many people in the West still use the Western models of leadership, but now people have realized that this method is not sufficient in the times of globalization. This is why many organizations nowadays try to accommodate cultural differences and are trying to incorporate different approaches to leadership. It has now become crucial for managers to learn how to adapt to their surroundings and circumstances.

Leading employees from different cultural backgrounds have become an everyday challenge for a lot of leaders. Cultural differences and how they work in-group as well as personal relationships have now become especially crucial.

Local cultures can significantly change the definition, as well as the application of leadership methods.

It is important to understand the historical development of the traditions in different nations.

For leaders who are supposed to manage global teams, it is recommended to get acquainted with the cultures of the members. It will allow you to understand their behavior and what sort of leadership will work the best with them. If leaders go the extra mile in the beginning, they will not have to face any other significant problems in the future. It is necessary to get acquainted with the local environment and cultural aspects as well. However, avoid going 'native'. This will make you seem less authentic, and people will think that you are trying to appropriate their culture. It is recommended to avoid the behavior of the locals. Instead of doing this, try to understand the cultural practices and act as authentic as possible.

Chapter 7 How Great Leaders Inspire Action/ The 7 Great Leadership Traits

The Mandate of Heaven

The "Mandate of Heaven" is an ancient philosophical concept that originated in China in the Zhou Dynasty around the year (1046-256 BCE) According to the Mandate, the Emperor of China was supposed to be virtuous enough to rule. If the Emperor were not able to fulfill the obligations of the emperor, then he would lose the Mandate and thus the right to be the Emperor.

Construction of Mandate

The Mandate was constructed using the following four principles:

1.   Heaven gives the Emperor the right to rule.
2.   As there exists only one Heaven, so there can be only one Emperor
3.   The Emperor's virtues make him capable of ruling.
4.   None of the dynasties can rule permanently.

There are various examples when the Emperor lost the Mandate of Heaven due to reasons such as invasions, peasant uprisings, famine, droughts, earthquakes, and floods. Floods and droughts both lead to famines that ultimately lead to peasant uprisings. Thus, most of the above reasons were interconnected.

Although the Mandate of Heaven sounds sort of similar to the concept of the 'Divine Right of Kings' in Europe, it operated in a much different way. In the European model, a particular family was granted the right to rule by God. The Right would never change even if the ruler's behavior were seen to be preposterous. This is why we have many examples of incompetent and insane European rulers. According to the Divine Right, no one could oppose the king, as it was a sin.

The Mandate of Heaven, however, justified rebellion against incompetent, tyrannical, or unjust rulers. If the rebellion was successful in overthrowing the ruler, then the Mandate was lost, and the leader of the rebels had gained it. The Mandate of Heaven was not hereditary like the Diving Right of Kings. It did not even care about royalty or royal birth. Anyone could become a Kind if they had the approval of Heaven.

The Mandate of Heaven in Action

The Mandate of Heaven was used to justify the overthrow of the Shang Dynasty by the Zhou Dynasty. Zhou leaders believed that the Shang emperors had become unfit of ruling because of rampant corruption.

After some years the Zhou dynasty crumbled but as there existed no opposition leader, a sort of Civil war begun in China. Ultimately the Qin Dynasty gained the Mandate but lost it soon. It was then gained by the Han Dynasty. This continued until the end of the Qing Dynasty in 1911.

Effects of the Idea

The Mandate of Heaven was considered to be highly important in China and neighboring countries, including Korea and Annam. As the rulers were afraid of losing the Mandate, they often carried out their duties in an honorary manner.

The Mandate also allowed social mobility, as even a peasant could become the emperor. It also gave a scapegoat for inexplicable events such as famines, droughts, floods, etc.

Machiavelli

A great and successful Machiavellian leader should possess five important traits. These traits decide whether a leader will be successful or not. These characteristics will be explained in detail below.

Fear

In medieval times, leaders believed that if their subjects were scared of them, they would not revolt. In today's society, this equation has changed significantly. For instance, nowadays, Presidents desire to love more than fear. This is especially true about democratic nations. If you decide that you want to be feared, it is necessary that your subjects should not hate you. There is a difference between hatred and fear. If people hate you, they will surely make schemes against you.

Support of the Governed

The second important trait that a successful leader must possess is the support of people. Without support, a leader cannot perform any actions. Machiavelli stresses the importance of people supporting the leader on almost every page of his book. Machiavelli believes that it is necessary for the leader to have support from the people because no military exercise can be successful without mercenary units. This means that you cannot expand your territory if you do not have people supporting you. You need to satisfy the basic needs of your people, or they will not support you.

Virtue

According to Machiavelli, a leader should either have virtue or should at least pretend to be virtuous. A virtuous leader can easily gain the support of people. It becomes easy for him or her to be in power for a long time. Machiavelli also says that having good virtues can hinder your rule, as it will limit your power significantly. For this Machiavelli suggests that the ruler should be virtuous in public and should do whatever is necessary to continue his rule in private.

Arms

Machiavelli believed that it is better to use your own forces instead of using mercenaries and other forces. Hiring soldiers can lead to a lot of negative results. If you hire your own people to fight for you, they will stay true to the cause until their last breath. Hired soldiers may flee when the times get tough. Auxiliary units are particularly bad because they will not be ready to die for you. This will make your army weak.

Intelligence

Intelligence is essential if you want to be a good leader. According to Machiavelli, intelligence is the most important trait that a successful leader must-have. Without intelligence, a King cannot rule and control people. He cannot gain the support of the people either. Intelligence helps the king to rule his territory with complete confidence. A King who depends on the decisions of his minister or assistant can be easily manipulated. It is always better to be smart and wise.

Napoleon

Napoleon is considered one of the greatest conquerors and leaders in the history of the modern world. Napoleon rose around the time of the French Revolution and changed French history forever.

During the peak of his reign, Napoleon controlled almost the whole of Europe. He was able to do so with the help of ambition, ingenuity, and cold-bloodedness.

History

Napoleon was born on the island of Corsica on 15 August 1769. When he was young, he was highly interested in warfare. Unsurprisingly, he went to a military college and studied warfare and became the 2nd Lieutenant in the artillery division.

France was going through a crisis around this time, which was soon followed by the French Revolution. Napoleon saw this and soon commanded the forces against tyranny and the British. He became a brigadier general at a young age.

Napoleon was ambitious right from his childhood, and thus he soon started attacking neighboring nations such as Russia, Italy, Austria, and Great Britain. Soon, he was captured almost the whole continent of Europe. But he was not able to conquer Russia or Great Britain. He suffered a heavy defeat in Moscow that was soon followed by a massive and career-ending defeat in the battle of Waterloo.

He was later exiled and passed away by stomach cancer on 5 May 1821. Some people believe that he was poisoned.

Leadership Lessons

Vision and Imagination

Napoleon is still praised for his exemplary vision and imagination. When he was the Emperor, he would win over men by showing how visionary he was. He would come up with various military tactics that were often way ahead of any other leaders of his time.

Thus, having a great vision is essential if you want to be a successful leader. A leader needs to know where he is leading his people. It is also recommended to share your vision with your employees as it will encourage and inspire them.

Know your folks

Napoleon understood that gaining the support of people was crucial. He would go around and know each of his soldiers by his name. This allowed him to establish personal contact with them.

People love to control the whole organization by sitting behind a table and directing orders through phone calls and emails. But organizations are often organic where you need to form bonds and connections if you want to be successful. Organizations are built upon relationships and establishing new and maintaining old relationships will make your organization grow. Take some time and get to know your team. Learn things about them and impress them.

Persistence is essential

If you want to be successful and victorious, you need to be persistent. You cannot achieve success if you are not dedicated and passionate about something. For instance, Napoleon was exiled, but he came back to take the throne of France.

Being consistent in your efforts will always help you to succeed. It is true that you may fail a couple of times in the beginning, but with time, dedication, and persistent, you will rise again and ultimately succeed.

Sun Tzu

In his seminal work The Art of War, Sun Tsu put forward the theory of leadership. According to him, a leader should possess five important traits. Let us have a look at these five traits, one by one.

Intelligence

If leaders want to succeed, they should be competent in every aspect of their work. They must exceed their own expectations if they want to become a great leader. They need to understand the needs of their colleagues. They need to understand their position in the organization as compared to the competitors. Leaders should understand how to take care of their intelligence. Boisterous leaders often fail.

Credibility

According to Sun Tzu, credibility is crucial if you want to be a great leader. Credibility comes from competence and trustworthiness. A leader should be able to display his experience, knowledge, and prowess.

Humaneness

Leaders should always be respectful of everyone. This includes everyone right from peers, subordinates, and even competitors. Great leaders understand that being humble will help them achieve great success. Humaneness is essential between leaders as well.

Leaders need to learn how to look at people as individuals and not just a team.

Courage

For Sun Tzu, a great leader is always courageous. He should be decisive and bold. The leader who bucks down due to pressure is not a great leader. Their judgment and prowess will be questioned by their peers and subordinates both. Courage enables leaders to take risks and find potential opportunities. Confidence and boldness provide a sense of credibility to his or her actions.

Discipline

According to Sun Tzu, a great leader is not only well trained, but he or she is also highly disciplined.

According to him, a leader should be ready all the time to fight in a battle. Leaders should evaluate situations and should never make rash decisions. This is often covered in their training. Discipline is learned and enforced through a complex and continuous system of punishments and rewards. Ultimately, for Sun Tzu, a leader needs to be bold and smart.

Conclusion

Thank you for buying this book! I hope you found it informative and interesting.

It is clear that leadership is one of the most crucial aspects of today's world. Today's world is highly focused on change and competition and to survive in this world, you need to adapt to change to quickly and be competitive as well. You also need to versatile, dedicated, and bold if you want to be a successful leader. Without this, no one can survive the trepidation of the modern corporate world. To become a great leader, you need to possess several qualities, all of which are related closely related to passion and strength of character. You cannot become a successful leader if you do not understand the contemporary world.

This book is a great guidebook that can help you become a great leader. It consists of various in-depth chapters that will help you become a successful leader. It opens with a chapter dealing with myths associated with leadership so that you can enter the world of development without any preconceived notions. An in-depth chapter dealing with different styles of leadership is one of the fortes of this book. It will allow you to understand which kind of leadership style you use and whether it is suitable for your workplace or not. It will also help you to make the necessary changes in your leadership style and adapt it according to your team. A chapter on various tips, tricks, and methods will help you to hone your leadership style and will make you a skillful leader. It will teach you how negativity and fear are two of the biggest enemies of a good leader. Some sections related to the barriers in leadership style and great historical leaders and their leadership style would help you understand what to do and what not to do while traversing the corporate world.

This book has covered almost everything that a leader needs to know to become a successful leader. In-depth chapters, well-researched topics, good examples, etc. all make this book one of the best leadership guides in the market. What makes it especially suitable for beginners is that it is written in a simple and lucid manner avoiding the complex jargon of the contemporary world. But this does not mean that it is not suitable for experts. The level of knowledge and information combined in this book will offer something to every reader-beginner or expert both.

While this book can help you become a great leader, it cannot work on its own. The clear message of this book is that if you want to be a great leader, you need to be dedicated and strong, and this book will help you to become so.

If you enjoyed this book and found some benefit in reading this, I'd like to hear from you and hope that you could take some time to post a review. Your feedback and support will help this author to greatly improve his writing craft for future projects and make this book even better.

Please keep in touch with me or for questions and advice: wswainpublishing@gmail.com

Thank you and good luck!

Peter Allen

References

http://blog.vernalmgmt.com/the-myth-of-innate-leadership/

https://www.forbes.com/sites/ekaterinawalter/2013/10/08/5-myths-of-leadership/#52872afe314e

https://www.thebalancecareers.com/common-myths-about-leadership-2275821

https://www.inc.com/mithu-storoni/these-5-rules-can-protect-your-team-from-toxic-negativity.html

https://yscouts.com/10-narcissistic-leadership-characteristics/

https://tomflick.com/2015/12/02/fear-vs-respect-why-leading-through-fear-is-never-the-answer/

https://www.psychologicalscience.org/news/minds-business/dominant-leaders-are-bad-for-groups.html

https://sites.psu.edu/leadership/2017/04/09/15415/

https://www.lollydaskal.com/leadership/7-powerful-habits-that-make-you-more-assertive/

https://www.forbes.com/sites/glennllopis/2013/05/20/6-effective-ways-listening-can-make-you-a-better-leader/#5af0213e1756

https://trainingindustry.com/blog/leadership/5-important-communication-skills-for-leaders/

https://www.fastcompany.com/3054067/7-habits-of-leaders-who-inspire-loyalty

https://www.n2growth.com/ceos-feared-or-respected/

https://www.businessinsider.com/how-to-be-a-leader-people-want-to-follow-2014-10?IR=T

https://hbr.org/2004/09/why-people-follow-the-leader-the-power-of-transference

https://www.thebalancecareers.com/developing-your-employees-2275869

https://studiousguy.com/paternalistic-leadership-style-types-examples/

https://www.eskill.com/blog/task-people-oriented-management/

https://www.verywellmind.com/what-is-democratic-leadership-2795315

https://www.verywellmind.com/what-is-laissez-faire-leadership-2795316

https://www.verywellmind.com/what-is-autocratic-leadership-2795314

http://www.leadershipexpert.co.uk/leadership-family.html

http://fltiofcolorado.colostate.edu/what-is-flti/what-is-family-leadership/

https://community.mbaworld.com/blog/b/weblog/posts/the-importance-of-self-leadership

https://www.brighthubpm.com/resource-management/93165-group-leadership-skills/

https://iedunote.com/management

http://www.yourarticlelibrary.com/organization/organization-meaning-definition-concepts-and-characteristics/53217

https://www.csoonline.com/article/2137088/the-anatomy-of-leadership---a-sun-tzu-perspective.html

http://www.leadershipgeeks.com/napoleon-leadership/

https://soapboxie.com/social-issues/Characteristics-of-a-Machiavellian-Leader

https://www.thoughtco.com/the-mandate-of-heaven-195113

https://www.ideasforleaders.com/ideas/leadership-beyond-the-western-model

https://en.wikipedia.org/wiki/Sex_differences_in_leadership

https://en.wikipedia.org/wiki/Self-monitoring

https://jenniferspoelma.com/blog-feed/what-is-self-efficacy-and-how-does-it-relate-to-leadership

https://aboutleaders.com/leadership-and-intelligence/#gs.m8qcln

http://theimportanceofemotionalintelligence.weebly.com/the-5-components.html

https://www.truity.com/book/big-five-personality-model

https://www.entrepreneur.com/article/312552

https://bizfluent.com/about-5445316-difference-between-male-female-leadership.html

Leadership 2.0

Leading Successful Teams, Businesses, Communications and Decisions Based on Neuroscience, Social Psychology and Leadership Principles

Peter Allen

Table of Contents

Introduction

"Leadership is simply causing other people to do what the leaders want. Good leadership, whether formal or informal, is helping other people rise to their full potential while accomplishing the mission and goals of the organization. All members of an organization, who are responsible for the work of others, have the potential to be good leaders if properly developed."

~ Bob Mason

Imagine a large, multinational corporation has just hired you as their new sales and marketing director in their international sales division. Global sales have been on a downward trend for several months, and you've been given what seems to be the impossible task of pulling an entire division back on track. You've hardly been given any information on your predecessor, your team, or your peers within the organization. All you know for sure is that there's a six-month window for you to prove yourself and implement positive change within the division. While six months sounds like enough time, you know you'll have to pull out all the stops if there's any hope of making it work.

Just then, the first signs of doubt and despair enter your mind. How are you going to succeed in turning an entire division around when you're not even sure what different types of personalities with which you're going to be working? You've already heard some water cooler gossip that staff is placing side bets on how long you're likely to last before you crack. Proving them wrong will be oh-so sweet, but how do you assume leadership of an entire department that's used to being crisis-managed?

Your brilliant track record in your previous company landed you this opportunity, but there, you were surrounded by friends and allies. You'd built solid relationships with your team and executive management. Questions begin swirling in your mind; Do you really have what it takes to lead them through this challenging period and onto bigger and better things? Will you be able to earn their trust and respect as a leader as quickly as possible? Can you shift the entire teams' focus onto areas of the business that are currently failing? Can you begin building a division all over again when you have no idea of what you're working with? It's more than just being able to identify the personality types and characteristics; it's a question of building trust, and doing it very quickly.

You can already feel the pressure of eyes watching every move you make from all sides. Your team isn't sure whether they can trust you or not, and those to whom you report have much higher expectations from the start. Your mandate requires you to ensure the sales division is operating like a well-oiled machine, or your head will be on the chopping block, and you know that you'll be facing the EXIT sign above the main entrance of the building.

You are already thinking of all the leadership skills you're not sure you currently possess, but you know they will be necessary if you'll be successful here. The first step is going to be earning the buy-in from those reporting to you, and gaining their trust as a leader. You know from experience that any insecurities or uncertainties displayed by you could be perceived as a weakness by the team. This may stand in the way of the entire department meeting goals set out by management. There's simply no way that you're going to allow this to happen during the six months you have. How do you meet these key objectives in any event? You know that there's no way to achieve this on your own.

Too many questions and uncertainties run through your mind, and you have so many decisions to face. Which do you tackle first, and how do you prove yourself to be a leader that a team wants to follow? Your management skills are sound because you've managed teams successfully in the past, but that was different. You'd been part of your previous firm for years, working your way up through the ranks and developing a reputation for yourself. You'd proven your worth to management and colleagues alike, and hit that glass ceiling where you could grow no further was devastating. You were looking for a bigger challenge, which is why you applied for this position; had you bitten off more than you can chew?

Admittedly, your management style and skills have not always been the greatest, and there has always been room for improvement. How could you learn to lead from the front when required, walk beside those that need guidance and direction, or gently nudge others from the back? Your stomach is in a knot, and you're beginning to feel overwhelmed. You don't know where to begin. You want to prove to the hiring manager and the management team that they made the right decision by bringing you on board, but it's going to mean learning as much about leadership as possible, and how to apply these skills to get the best out of your team.

Glancing over the motley crew, you're not even sure what personalities you've inherited or whether or not you'll be able to work with them. How can you determine where your current skills start and where they end? How can you learn to become a better leader, and to manage people better by empowering and inspiring them to be the very best they can be?

While this imaginary story may be applicable to someone who's already been a leader before, it may not apply to you. You may be wanting to get your feet wet and try your role at leadership, or you may be looking at studying towards becoming a leader someday. Wherever you find yourself, this book is for you. The following chapters are going to provide you with practical insights into leadership. What it is, and what it isn't. We will go through developing better relationships by connecting with people. After all, that's what leadership is all about. It will help you learn the art of effective communication with your team and those around you, so they'll follow you to the ends of the earth, no matter the cost. It will help you identify and enhance leadership skills you already possess and add those you still need.

This book is about learning to manage yourself first, managing others effectively, and learning to become a better leader. It's not just for all the leaders out there, it's also for supervisors, team leaders, managers, coaches, teachers, entrepreneurs, and employees—in short, this book is for anyone who would like to learn to strengthen their professional interpersonal relationships.

Some of the biggest challenges managers and leaders face in today's world is that they're qualified to supervise and lead on paper. They may have attended all the right training seminars and completed all the right courses, yet still don't possess the actual skills to lead. They don't know how to manage, motivate, and develop their employees. As individuals, they often stagnate in their roles, believing that 'once a leader, always a leader'. Rather than understanding that leadership is a skill that requires constant change, they become set in their ways.

This fast-paced world in which we live means that business is evolving and morphing at a frenetic pace. Leadership requires ongoing learning to ensure the best for those under you. Learning is not only necessary in times of crises, but rather should be a life-long commitment if you hold a leadership title. It's a way to embrace new technology and ideas, and should be seen as a means of strengthening teams and keeping abreast of innovative ways of doing things. It's keeping your finger on the pulse of all things "leadership" in your industry. Lack of learning results in stagnation, and no one flourishes or thrives under a stagnant leader.

Rapid changes across all industries result in many challenges for leaders, and while only a handful are listed below, you can understand why it's important to keep on top of whatever is happening within your industry. Most industries have their own unique set of challenges. Successful leaders can cut through all the bureaucratic red tape and get to the heart of the problem. The world of work has changed, and business is far from a time when men clocked in at the beginning of the day, reporting to their small cubicle, putting their heads down and working only to punch out at the end of the day, repeating the cycle all over again the following day. The humdrum boring monotony of this environment was what defined the world of work in the past, but it's most certainly not how things work today.

Now you have somewhat of an alphabet soup as various generations make up most of the workforce, and it's not only their outlook that's different. Gone are the days of the typical nine to five work routine with men in bowler hats and grey suits reporting for duty, never questioning anything because they were just happy to have work and receive a steady paycheck at the end of each month. Because of this, it makes perfect sense that the way people are led and managed should also undergo similar changes to meet the demands of the new world of work.

For the silent generation and baby boomers, most employees began and ended their careers within the same organization, retiring with their neatly packaged 401K and a gold pocket watch for 40 years of service. Millennials currently represent the largest workforce globally, and companies are being challenged in finding innovative ways to keep them. This turnover alone costs organizations and economies millions annually. This largest generation is constantly open to bigger and better things, so how do you learn to retain them and engage them?

Leadership skills are essential for everyone, and the great news is that it can be learned, meaning that there's no excuse for poor leadership. If leadership issues appear, they can be rectified and strengthened, rather than assuming that individuals are bad leaders. It's more cost-effective to identify areas of leadership that need to be strengthened and work on those, rather than disrupting entire departments or teams.

Thanks to emotional intelligence (EQ), we begin to understand ourselves and those around us better, which is crucial to leadership. You cannot expect others to follow you to where you have not been, or are unwilling to go on your own. Making use of emotional intelligence as part of your leadership strategy is another way to play to the strengths of individuals on your team.

There are many different styles of leadership to learn today, and just as many points of view. If you were to stop and ask 50 different individuals on the street, or run a snap survey within your organization, you're likely to find around 50 different answers to the same question. As a leader, you should remain as true to your natural leadership style as possible, if it's both effective and beneficial to your team and the company. If it isn't, then learning from a book like this can teach you how to make small adjustments to influence the lives of those you supervise in positive ways. This will impact the overall bottom-line of the business. Happy employees are productive employees. They are loyal employees and will give you everything they have. As their leader, recognition for great work should form part of your leadership strategy.

As a leader, personal goals are important. Set goals to learn new leadership skills to make your methods more effective. Strive to be liked and trusted by those reporting to you. Once you achieve this, you'll not only see better results from your team, but you can improve your retention strategies. Organizations with high staff turnover can end up spending millions of dollars retraining new hires and getting them up to speed. A happy staff is a productive staff, and teams collaborate better in this environment.

The main purpose of this book is to teach you how to master leadership skills that will motivate and inspire you and your team toward success. It's important to be able to define your department's organizational objectives—where are you going? How are you planning on getting there? And more importantly, why are you planning on moving in that direction? When individuals understand why they're doing something, they're more likely to buy-in and follow you. If they're left in the dark, then that's pretty much where they're likely to stay... in the dark, floundering!

Too many books about leadership are boring, repetitive, and the same as the rest. In this book, we will look towards providing you with concise, powerful, no-nonsense advice. The information is based on personal experience, research ranging from neuroscience, to science, to social psychology, and is backed up by scientific statistical data or analysis.

As you begin to improve and master your leadership skills, you will begin to see results from your colleagues. They will begin to trust you more and will follow you, doing whatever necessary to ensure objectives are met. Where you once may have doubted your abilities, you will feel more confident than ever before, and this will be seen within the relationships you have with those reporting to you.

This book is a must-read for all leaders, no matter the industry or leadership situation you find yourself in. Even as a parent, you will benefit from the information on these pages. There's not a moment to waste in deciding what you want from your life. Are you happy to stick with mediocrity and passing the time, or are you ready to kickstart your leadership style to the next level?

The choice now lies in your hands. Think about it. Where do you want to be a year from now? Do you want to be recognized as a leader that is on top of his or her game, changing things from the inside out? Or do you want to be left where you are now—still struggling to come to terms with what you could have, would have, or should have done? Are you ready to face defeat, refusing to grow as a leader, or are you prepared to dive into the following chapters, making each one of them your own? I look forward to having you join me, Peter Allen, author and business leader, on this life-altering leadership journey!

Chapter 1: Leadership Model

Unpacked

"The single biggest way to impact an organization is to focus on leadership development. There is almost no limit to the potential of an organization that recruits good people, raises them up as leaders and continuously develops them."

~ John C. Maxwell

The Model

The model that this book will follow is based on research from various scientific fields that have conducted extensive studies on leadership. Much has changed since the early 1900s, when behavioral science and psychology were all the rage. We are briefly going to consider some of the most influential psychologists who shaped leadership theories and are often referred to as the 'founding fathers' of behavioral science. Not all their theories were accurate or workable, and along with changes in the world of work, many of these psychologists altered their own opinions. Psychologists such as Freud, Thomas Carlyle, and many others had varying opinions on the subject, and as a result, streamlined the process of what it's become today. What few individuals consider, however, is that given the definition of leadership, many leaders existed throughout the period. Turning to history, one needs to consider individuals such as Caesar, Cleopatra, Genghis Khan, Alexander the Great, and Tutankhamen. At the time, these individuals were not always seen to be great leaders, although they led hundreds of thousands of individuals collectively. Much of their leadership characteristics were fear-based, rather than caring about the welfare of their people. (Maybe this is one of the reasons why they were born to lead during the eras they did.)

Working hand-in-hand with science is a way to identify certain leadership qualities, or strengths that an individual may have, yet these are not the final predictor as to whether or not you will be successful in a leadership role. There's much more to leadership than possessing great communication skills.

Despite some of the best possible predictive assessments, there is and always will be the human element involved in each leader, making it extremely difficult to put every single character in their own separate neat and tidy box. Statistical data analysis, whether strength and weakness-based, or gathered using longitudinal models, has been applied to the field of leadership for many decades. In keeping with this information, most of what we present will be based on these same models, in a concise way that offers you powerful, and applicable advice. Rather than skimming the surface, we will focus on those areas that will provide you with a better understanding of how your thoughts, decisions, and actions affect each of us as leaders in the 21st century. We will also consider areas where you may currently have limitations as a means of improving in these areas and turning each limitation into a strength. While this may sound like this is quite a simple process, it's not. Some limitations could take years to turn around. Being aware of them is an excellent place to start.

What is Leadership?

According to the Oxford online dictionary, 'leadership' is defined by the following words: authority, control, direction, guidance, influence, initiative, management, and supervision (Oxford, 2020).

Another definition that best describes it is by leadership expert, John C. Maxwell. He states in his bestselling book, *The 21 Irrefutable Laws of Leadership: Follow them and people will follow you*, that "The true measure of leadership is influence. Nothing more, nothing less" (Maxwell, 1998/2000). Being able to influence others and obtain followers could either be positive or negative, depending on who's doing the leading. Almost every industry has their own unique set of rules that govern the type of leadership they want. For the purpose of this book, we will look at leadership in business.

For most, it's the ability to lead others to achieve a set of goals or objectives that have been outlined by the company. It may be providing assistance and direction on how to get from one place to another, or being able to motivate a group of individuals towards common goals within an organization. While most are under the impression that you need a piece of paper, neatly framed, hanging behind your desk in a corner office before you are qualified to lead others, nothing could be further from the truth.

You can lead those around you purely through influence, rather than having to pressurize them to accept your way or the highway. There's more to leadership than meets the eye, and it's often easier to allow others to be in front.

It's more than learning to accept all the glory when things go right, and chastising others when things go wrong. A true leader gives credit where it's due, and then some. They get to know their team, discovering each's strengths and limitations and learning how to best work with them. Genuine leaders take an interest in the overall personal growth and development of their subordinates, or those for which they're responsible. They know how to accept blame when things go wrong and continue to keep their team motivated.

Being a leader means that you never have to make excuses for why things are not working out quite the way you would have liked them to. It's being able to analyze what went wrong along the way and gently guiding people back to where they need to be, helping them every step of the way. It's providing an open door, a listening ear, a shoulder to lean on, and the voice of reason when necessary. Leadership is being able to foresee things before they happen and doing whatever is required to prevent catastrophic fallout.

It does not mean giving in or caving at the first sign of opposition or defeat. Instead, it's about learning to stand your ground and standing up for those for which you're responsible, even though they may be in the wrong. It's giving them the benefit of the doubt first, and learning to help them through any periods where they may need to further learn and grow.

Leadership is about identifying and nurturing the talent within those individuals for which you're responsible. This means developing relationships with them where they are prepared to be open and honest with you at all times. They need to be willing to communicate with you openly and honestly. Rather than raising your own status above theirs as a leader, win them over to your side. If you attempt to rule over them, they will begin to create barriers between you and your team, and it's usually a long way back before you can guarantee cooperation and understanding. You want to be able to collaborate with everyone in your circle of influence.

Leadership is not about standing behind people, barking down orders with a bullhorn in one hand. It's not about the title that sits behind or beneath your name. Almost every organization like yours has similar management structures, so there are many others in the world carrying the same title as you. You don't even need a title to be an effective leader. Anyone can shout out orders to their workers and get fear-based results. That's not to say that you're getting the very best of what the employees are able to give you, or according to their individual capacity.

Stop reading for a few minutes and think about everyone in your department, your division, your branch, or your business? How much do you really know about each of them? Do you know what their greatest goals in life are? Do you even know what their ambitions within your organization are? Widen your outlook further, considering other divisions. Do you know your peers and co-workers? How about those that are on the same level as you? Do you know what their long- or short-term goals and aspirations are? Do you even know their names? While this may be a virtual impossibility for large organizations, small to medium enterprises should not have these problems. If you are meeting with your management team regularly, or even if you happen to sit on an Executive Committee at the Board level, it's still important to know what makes each of your colleagues get up and at it every day.

Being a leader is more than just picking up a larger paycheck than those you're responsible for—it's doing exactly that. Being responsible for them. Let's face it, it's easier to assume responsibility for others, genuine responsibility, only once you know them. Without this, it's merely posturing. It's putting on an act, playing a game, wearing a mask for the sake of either the 'higher-ups', or confusing yourself into thinking that you care.

Being a leader is not about pointing out faults and failures all day long. Instead, it's about working collectively towards uniting and strengthening individuals. The old saying, "you catch more flies with honey than with vinegar" springs to mind.

Being a leader doesn't mean that you get to bully others with scare tactics or threats; while it may be seen as a position of power, it should be one of humility instead. You should be acutely aware of your own shortcomings and failures and work on those. It's not always necessary to let your team in on these limitations, however, at times, that may be exactly what's required for them to be more tolerant, or cohesive. It may help them work together towards the achievement of common goals because they accept and understand that you, as an individual, are also human, with faults and failures, much the same as everyone else. It could help humanize you to them, instead of the rift between management and employees, that gap could be made much smaller.

So, how do you go about determining what type of leader you are, and how this is possibly going to assist you in your day-to-day working life? The first thing you need to do is take a long hard look in the mirror and identify those areas of your leadership style, and whether these are working with you, for you, or against you. Are there areas that need to be addressed and attended to? What are they? And what do you need to change to become the type of leader you would like to be?

Is your position within your organization and level of seniority a threat to you? Has it gone to your head? Has your senior management team assumed that you would magically find all the answers to be an effective leader just because you were promoted? (It's much the same argument as having the qualification and automatically assuming that this is going to make you an excellent leader).

Is leadership just for those in executive positions? Or can you become an effective leader right where you are (without a fancy promotion or pay increase)?

What You Need to Become A Leader

For psychologist and author, Kendra Cherry, and psychotherapist and author of *13 Things Mentally Strong People Don't Do*, Amy Morin, the following things should be accomplished in order to become a leader:

• The first and most important step when it comes to effective leadership is identifying and understanding your leadership style. Without this, it's impossible to know what your strengths and limitations are. In leadership, you need to be able to play to your strengths and look towards overcoming your limitations.

- Actively listen to those you supervise and communicate effectively with them.

- Be a positive role model and encourage those you lead to be innovative and creative. Help them discover how to think for themselves and "outside the box" rather than being another version of you.

- Be passionate about the work that you do, and through your positive attitude towards what needs to be done, encourage the participation of those you lead.

- Use rewards and recognition to motivate and encourage active participation from those within your team (Cherry & Morin, 2019).

How to Approach Leadership

According to Rita Balian Allen, a lecturer at Northeastern University, and Top Ten Executive Leadership Coaches in the USA, there are many different styles or approaches to leadership today. While there's no "one-size-fits-all" approach to leadership, it appears that the most prominent styles of leadership can be divided into five divisions. In a recent interview with Leslie Doyle, a writer from the University, she had these important points to say about leadership (Doyle, 2019). We will focus each of these in this section:

Participatory Leadership

This was previously referred to as a democratic leadership style, where employees are very much part of the decision-making process. As a participatory leader, a hands-on approach is adopted, and employees are recognized for the value they bring to the organization. These leaders encourage participation from their employees, allowing them to have a say in decisions and the way things are run. It's completely different from a regular "top-down" leadership strategy. An example of this type of leader is Martha Stewart and Donald Trump (Malsam, 2019).

Servant Leadership

This is the youngest of the different leadership styles and strategies. Servant leaders are more concerned with doing what's right for their workforce than what's right for them. They are focused on the needs of their people and building each employee as an individual by doing what's right for the team, individuals, and the community. They place themselves last, rather than first. This term was first coined by Robert K. Greenleaf in 1970. Well-known servant leaders include Steven Covey and Ken Blanchard (Wilbanks, 2018).

Studies have confirmed that this style of leadership yields higher returns and employees perform much better in this environment.

Situational Leadership

Developed by Ken Blanchard and Paul Hersey in 1969, they describe situational leaders as those who are able to assess the strengths of those within their team and to assign them tasks in line with their abilities. Communication between team members and leaders is essential for this type of leadership to be successful. Situational leaders manage their team according to strengths, limitations, and their motivations. Advancements within the team inspire individuals to perform better (Cherry & Morin, 2019).

Transformational Leadership

This type of leadership believes in increasing morale within a team and encouraging performance through connection. It's important for team members to be able to connect with the organization, as well as their own identities. Examples of transformational leaders include Winston Churchill and Steve Jobs.

Value-based Leadership

These leaders encourage members of their team to work towards the greater good of the shared values within an organization. This encourages teams to focus on the mission and vision of an organization, rather than following blindly. The leader themselves would uphold each of these core values, which would be built around the same values of the organization.

Can You Learn to Be a Good Leader?

There are so many ways to learn good leadership skills in this modern society, and yes, these skills can certainly be learned. Some of the basics could range from making a genuine impact on the lives of those you manage, to not showing favoritism among those you lead. According to Walden University, here are a few of their recommendations when learning to become a more effective leader:

• Don't be afraid to display the passion you have for what you do. Far too many leaders really love their work, yet they don't want their team, or those around them, to see it. You don't need to love absolutely everything about what you do to be passionate. Discover those facets of your work that you thoroughly enjoy doing, and focus your passion there. You can always build on it later.

• Good leaders realize that it's not about being popular all the time—they make hard decisions at the risk of being viewed as tough or unpopular. They know that there's no popularity contest when it comes to doing the right thing. And they choose to do the right thing every time, no matter how others feel about it.

• They're open to new ideas—the current market and world of work in which we live are forever changing, and it's only so long before another change comes along, as part of a natural way of doing things. They understand that their answers aren't always the right ones, and that's why they like to hear what others have to say so the best decisions are made, rather than the first decision, which may not be the best for all concerned.

• They adopt servant leadership skills and work for the good of their employees, rather than selfishly for themselves. Despite having to report to their manager(s), they strive to make the lives of their team better. This is done by creating an environment conducive to helping their employees to thrive. Happy employees are loyal and productive employees.

• They remain positive towards their staff, leading from the front. This means that they coach and support team members during difficult times, they praise their employees for positive contributions towards their work, and they stand by them when things are tough. Good leaders don't flip-flop between support, being supportive at certain times, and then changing whenever it suits them.

• Good leaders are respectful. They don't choose who they are going to respect. Some leaders are only respectful towards those to whom they report, while treating their employees poorly, as they decide to pull the "management" card. Good leaders respect both those above them, as well as those they lead.

• From the get-go, good leaders set the right example for their team to follow. They understand that leadership is not about them. Whenever something needs to be done, they will be the first to arrive in the morning, and usually be the last to leave at the end of the day. They don't expect their employees to do anything they're not prepared to do themselves.

• They accept that learning is a lifelong pursuit and do this not only by setting the right example for their team, but also encouraging team members to do the same. Most large organizations are prepared to invest in their employees to become better at what they do. If this is the situation within your organization, embrace these opportunities with both hands, and look for learning opportunities that will further your advancement within the organization. Learning is for everyone and should be treated that way (Walden University Blog, n.d.).

Chapter 2: Leadership Defined

"A true leader has the confidence to stand alone, the courage to make tough decisions, and the compassion to listen to the needs of others. He does not set out to be a leader but becomes one by the equality of his actions and the integrity of his intent."

~ Douglas MacArthur

Characteristics of Leaders

According to the Center for Creative Research, there are 10 characteristics that every successful leader possesses (Center for Creative Leadership Blog, 2019). They are:

The Art of Delegation

Being able to delegate is an important skill for any leader to master as early in their career as possible. This will help alleviate pressure when you have deadlines looming by sharing the workload between members of your team. Delegation is not passing your specific work onto other people. Instead, it's sharing a collective, team-based workload. When the entire team gets involved, relationships are strengthened. It allows your team to get to see who you are and understand you better, helping them realize that you are also human, just like them, and have days when pressure can build up. Opening up to your team through task delegation builds trust and mutual respect. You, as their leader, need to learn that you can trust them to complete whatever you assign them. You need to take opportunities that will help you to foster relationships, allowing them to work without being micromanaged. It lets them see that they are part of something bigger, a team that's valued, rather than a smaller cog in an organizational wheel.

Communicate Effectively

Communication is covered extensively in the final chapter. In terms of key ingredients to successful leadership in the 21st century, it's a vital ingredient.

Stand Up For Your Team

It takes tremendous courage to lead from the front. Even when you fear failure or ridicule, you need to stand up for yourself and your team. Fear often holds us back and can prevent us from achieving our goals as leaders, or collectively as a team. Many leaders ignore whatever negative or unhealthy things happening in their department in the hope that they will resolve themselves. This is the exact opposite of what courageous leaders need to be doing. Leaders should do more than bury their heads in the sand like an ostrich, and help resolve disputes, problems, and hiccups in the workplace before they are blown out of proportion. Fear makes these situations much worse than they need to be. As a leader, it is your job to step out of your comfort zone and be prepared to defend yourself, your team, your colleagues, or even your organization, no matter the cost.

Understanding Others

Having empathy towards those reporting to you, and learning to understand them is a key skill associated with emotional intelligence (EQ), and can be learned. Displaying these feelings in the workplace does not make you weak; it makes you human. It allows employees to see another side of you, one that cares what's happening in their lives and/or in the workplace. If you always expect your employees to give their best, this is a skill you need to practice and learn to master if you're not using it as a leadership technique already.

The Center of Creative Leadership completed a study by collecting and analyzing data from 6,731 managers in 38 countries. The purpose of the study was "to determine whether empathy can influence a manager's job performance." The results proved that those managers who displayed empathy towards their subordinates in the workplace were viewed by their own managers as being better performers. Emotional intelligence is all about our ability to connect. Using empathy and compassion allows you to understand and try to identify with the other individual's thoughts and feelings (Center of Creative Leadership Articles, n.d.-b).

Be aware of confusing empathy with sympathy. Sympathy is pitying someone without trying to place yourself in their shoes. Seeking understanding rather than proclaiming judgment is what you're aiming for as a leader. Learn to be truly present and pay close attention when employees are discussing problems with you.

Being Grateful

Too few leaders express sincere gratitude towards their employees for things such as work done, ideas shared, and putting in extra hours when not asked to do so to reach a deadline. Instead, leaders assume it's part of their work responsibility. While this may be true to a degree, in the sense that the employee is collecting a check at the end of every month, all the little extras are often what makes the difference. As a leader, saying thank you can lead to less stress and anxiety in the workplace, and greater self-esteem in your employees (Center for Creative Leadership Articles, n.d.-a).

There's a science behind expressing gratitude that goes hand-in-hand with both happiness and an overall sense of well-being. A controlled trial tested for connections between gratitude, sleep patterns, and subjective well-being. The trial was conducted using 119 young women over two weeks. Those randomly selected were asked to give thanks or express gratitude over the two-week period. The balance was requested to report on everyday events that occurred in their lives. At the end of this period, results indicated that sleep patterns improved, test subjects enjoyed an overall decrease in blood pressure. It further established that expressing gratitude was not only beneficial to the individual giving thanks, but also to the recipient (Jackowska et al., 2016).

A survey conducted by Glassdoor indicated that 80% of employees would work much harder in the workplace if their leader was more appreciative toward them and expressed gratitude. (Glassdoor Team, 2013).

Influence versus Control

Effective leadership is being able to influence others to do whatever is necessary while not trying to control them. As another EQ skill, it means that you should be able to connect with those reporting to you. Influence is the exact opposite of control or manipulation. It's not forcing your employees into subdued compliance, but convincing them to do things by choice on their own. It's allowing employees the freedom to follow, having built trust between you. George Hallenbeck, from the Center of Creative Leadership and the main contributor of their "Lead 4 Success" program says that "Without the ability to influence the heads, hearts, and hands of people, the truly important things in work and in life can't be achieved." (Center for Creative Leadership Articles, 2017). He goes on to identify the following four key skills:

Use Network Connections: You must have the ability to be able to network and connect with others, and then be able to make use of these networks in your favor.

Work Towards Common Goals: Understand how to get individuals moving towards common goals because they want to, not because they're being forced to.

<u>Team Collaboration</u>: Use authenticity and credibility to do what's best for the company. The organizational needs should always come first, above any personal agendas.

<u>Influence with Trust</u>: Use trust and influence to lead and direct individuals and teams. You can only achieve these things once your team trusts you and is ready to follow you wherever you lead them.

Honesty and Integrity

It feels as though this section should not have to be included, because as a leader, these two closely intertwined characteristics should come as a given. Unfortunately, not all leaders have unquestionable honesty and integrity. Leaders are responsible for the direction entire organizations move in, as well as what seems like an endless supply of other important business decisions. Integrity should be the first box to be checked off during an initial hiring interview. Not just for employees, but for every individual within an organization. The higher up the rung of the corporate ladder, the greater the level of honesty and integrity should be.

It's unsurprising, in the world in which we currently live, that dishonesty and scandal are found almost everywhere you look. Once again, studies have shown that for senior executives within organizations, "Integrity [is] the most important [strength] for top-level executives' performance" (Center for Creative Leadership Articles, n.d.-c).

Integrity is choosing to do the right thing even when nobody is watching you. It's being 100% trustworthy and ensuring your word is your bond. It's deciding what's right and what's wrong early in your life, and then never deviating into the murky depths of grey. As a leader, this should be unquestionable. As someone responsible for hiring those below you, if you use this as your standard, you should never have to question the integrity of anyone in your team.

Increased Learning Agility

Part of being a leader in the 21st century is recognizing that changes and advancements are going to require unlearning the old and relearning the new. Being able to tap into this skill is what's referred to as "learning agility." According to Megha Singh from the Learning and Development Division of Mecer,

"Learning agility is the ability to continually and rapidly learn, unlearn, and relearn mental models and practices from a variety of experiences, people, and sources, and to apply that learning in new and changing contexts to achieve desired results. It is a mind-set and corresponding collection of practices that allow people to continually develop, grow, and utilize new strategies that will equip them for the increasingly complex problems they face in their organizations."

In his 1970s book, *Future Shock*, Alvin Toffler made the following quotation that was way ahead of its time when he said, "The illiterate of the 21st century will not be those who cannot read and write, but those who cannot learn, unlearn and relearn" (Toffler, 1970).

Those who are especially good at embracing learning agility are usually more actively involved in what's happening within their organization. They are able to come up with new ideas fairly quickly, and don't have problems implementing solutions that work. In addition to the above, they come off as being more resilient and calm in the workplace. As leaders within this type of environment, they not only encourage their staff to become involved in learning agility behavior, but they also provide various solutions where their employees can benefit from this extra learning.

• The benefits of learning agility include improved productivity within the various departments and the organization as a whole.

• There's an increase in the number of employees who are ready to face whatever challenges are thrown their way as part of changes within the workplace.

• Why is learning agility necessary for today's workplace?

There are technological advancements taking place that are shaping the future of the world of work at the moment. This means advancements in artificial intelligence (AI) and robotics; technological advancements require constant innovation and having to reinvent not only business models, but often entire positions within business. This is thanks to a marketplace that is currently expanding due to globalization (this brings its own specific highly competitive dynamic with it).

Millennials, who make up the largest population of the current workforce, are constantly rebelling against the old way of doing things. They not only want to work differently, but demand that the entire work landscape changes to suit their specific needs. Naturally, within the workplace, the division bearing the brunt of all these changes is Human Resources (HR). They not only need to look for those who display the potential to be able to learn, unlearn, and relearn, but also those who can get along with others (Singh, 2020).

Four steps that can be taken to approach learning agility are:

Looking: Finding the right place to gain the knowledge or skills required to complete future tasks.

Understanding Learning: It's not just important to find where to acquire these new skills or knowledge, but you need to understand what you are learning. This can be done by questioning things you don't understand until you reach a point where you do.

Internalizing Learning: Make whatever you've learned your own. This key component to learning agility will help you to move onto the following step!

Application of New Learning: The point of learning new skills can only be valuable if you can apply what you've been taught. It should allow you to improve your current working environment, whether this means improving on processes, or working better with your team. Whatever new skill you are fortunate enough to learn or relearn needs to be applied. If it so happens that you were the only individual within your team fortunate enough to attend a training environment, share the knowledge gained with your team.

The entire emphasis of learning agility is to make things better for everyone. By sharing with your team, there will always be someone within your inner circle in the workplace who can back you up, or help out if you aren't there for some reason. Learning agility should be a skill adopted by everyone, and not just shared with a select few.

Admiration and Respect

In this context, we are discussing the leaders' respect for those they lead. While respect is often referred to as a two-way street, as their leader, you cannot expect your employees to deliver their best work if they feel that you don't respect them as individuals or collectively as a team. There are many ways you can show your employees that you respect them, or that they're valued members of the team as a collective group of individuals. For teams to work more effectively as a cohesive unit, they need to feel your support as their leader. They also need to feel that they are respected and supported as part of a team. Here are some ways that you, as their leader, can physically show this support:

• Having an open-door policy when teams are working on projects. Indicate that you are available to assist in any way you possibly can. It's important that you actually mean this, and aren't just paying them lip-service.

• Providing an environment where you're prepared to listen to what your team has to say. This is more than pretending to listen and be concerned. It's allowing your employees to use you as a sounding board to bounce ideas off of. It's recognizing them for their input as part of the team, and the entire team's participation when it comes to projects. A practical tip, when it comes to active listening, is to allow the other person to finish speaking first, before interrupting with an answer.

Learning to trust your team is another way to show your respect for them. According to Social-Emotional Intelligence and Soft-Skills Training expert, Stefan Jacobson, the most important time to be honest and open with your team is when you need to provide feedback that's not always comfortable. Times like these are never easy, however, they are necessary for teams and individuals alike to be able to grow (Jacobson, 2019).

Jacobson also states that one of the most effective ways to show respect towards your employees is by encouraging them to participate in important projects and providing them with honest feedback. Not everyone is prepared to leave their comfort zones to step out of the shadows that they're used to. Often, team members are happy to keep their heads down without anyone even noticing them. They fly under the radar constantly, remaining silent in company meetings, even preferring to hide behind their colleagues. What's often sad about these individuals is they are highly intelligent and could have a lot to contribute. Encourage them to participate in group discussions. Make them feel comfortable and confident. As you do so, they will feel more inclined to contribute again in the future.

Self-awareness

Self-awareness is another EQ-based leadership skill, although it's one that's inward-facing. This means that rather than considering what's happening around you, you need to be in touch with your thoughts and feelings instead. According to Michelle Kankousky from the Learning and Development Consultant for Insperity, there are several strategies that you can incorporate into your leadership strategy that deal with self-awareness. Some of these are (Kankousky, 2017):

Understanding Your Strengths and Weaknesses: This is never a comfortable subject to have to face, yet we all have both strengths and weaknesses. The idea when working with self-awareness is to learn how to play to your strengths and overcome your weaknesses at the same time. This is easier said than done, of course (if you've ever tried to overcome a weakness or limitation, you know what I mean). It's only through understanding these and identifying possible triggers that you can begin to overcome them one at a time.

Ask for Feedback: As important as it is for you, as a leader, to provide your team with both positive and negative feedback for them to grow, invite them to provide you with feedback on your leadership. Remember that once you do this, you should be prepared for the occasional negative feedback, and accept it without bitterness and bias. Afterall, you want to improve as a leader—and this is how you do it. Feedback could also come from your peers and those above you. It's also recommended that this happens more often than an annual review. If there are specific areas you need to change, it's better knowing about them as soon as possible.

Be Open-Minded: This is an excellent way to get to know your team better and to really learn to collaborate more effectively. If you are one of these leaders that likes everything to be just perfect before moving ahead with a project, you are going to (and probably have) face a lot of disappointments in your life. Keep an open mind with your team. Allow them to contribute and share their ideas during brainstorming or problem-solving sessions. Consider how each individual team member operates and plays to their strengths. Although you are the leader, the group as a whole should come first.

Chapter 3: Leading Yourself

"Control is not leadership; management is not leadership; leadership is leadership. If you seek to lead, invest at least 50% of your time in leading yourself—your own purpose, ethics, principles, motivation, conduct. Invest at least 20% leading those with authority over you and 15% leading your peers."

~ Dee Hock

Set the Example

Good leaders set the example for those reporting to them to follow. As they do, they allow those they lead to learn from them and inspire them to be better in their own jobs. Leaders understand that team(s) are watching them, manager(s) are watching them, and it would be unreasonable to expect others to follow you if you're not prepared to lead by example. Setting this example means putting in extra hours whenever necessary without moaning or complaining. It's setting the right example in every area of the job.

Make sure your team can see you and knows what you are doing. If you're putting in extra hours, be sure they're aware that you're prepared to do this and are doing it for the benefit of the team. This shouldn't be done in a way that makes them feel inferior. Instead, invite them to join in these activities, making it easier for them to follow you as a leader.

Leaders aren't afraid of helping team members feeling overwhelmed with their workloads. This forms part of servant leadership. If others realize you see what's happening in your department and aren't afraid of assisting if there's a major project that needs working on, the more they will be inclined to help one another.

Why do you want to set an example of leadership for those in your team to follow? Do you want greater influence over them, popularity, or do you have selfish motives? In leadership, there will always be someone watching everything you do. While it may not always be the same individual doing the watching, someone is noticing the hours you put in, the number of coffee breaks you take, the way you dress, how you address your superiors and your subordinates—everything is being watched and analyzed. You may even be the owner of the organization and feel that because of this designation, you should be precluded from this kind of scrutiny. Unfortunately, in this instance, you are probably scrutinized even more carefully, and not just by individuals within your own organization.

Setting the right example needs to be visible. Without it, what's the point of doing the work if nobody can see what you're doing? As a leader, your team of employees should recognize your contributions towards the team. Something to remember as a leader is that actions can have a far greater impact than words ever could.

Learn from Experience

Criticism and Advice

Accepting advice or criticism can be tough since most of the time, we believe we're right. Becoming a leader isn't achieved automatically or overnight. You cannot step into a leadership role and get everything 100% right the first time. Remember what it felt like receiving sage advice from those who were more experienced in management than you? Hold onto those feelings. If you were fortunate enough to have a mentor or a career coach that helped you through your early leadership years, remember how much of that learning was by trial and error. If you're a brand new leader, please understand that coping with advice and criticism is a skill that you will need to develop, but it's one you will use throughout your life, because you will never please everyone all the time. Focus on how you can improve and ask for feedback from those who are older and wiser than you (this is not necessarily an age dynamic, look for those who have more leadership experience). Receiving this advice will keep you on your toes and continue to move forward, rather than stagnating as a leader and accepting the status quo as good enough.

Additional Workload

Do you recall when you first had additional responsibilities added to your leadership role and how this made you feel? That sense of being overwhelmed, unsure of which task needed to be managed first? Tap into these memories and how you handled the situation. This is not to say that the way you dealt with it was always the best. What is undeniable, however, is that you gained valuable knowledge and experience from it and this allowed you to learn.

Part of being a successful leader means being flexible, willing, and able to deal with whatever is thrown your way without flinching or losing sight of the end goal. How you react to your supervisors' requests to take on extra work is exactly how your team will react when you assign additional work to them. Learning coping skills is part of a learning curve, without collapsing into a heap feeling overstressed, overworked, or wanting to throw a pity-party because you're feeling underappreciated. Instead, use this to your advantage by delegating additional work to your team, while closely monitoring them so they don't feel the same way you did the first time it happened to you.

Feedback

Apart from asking members of your team for regular feedback, ask clients by interacting with them. This could provide, not only you, but your entire organization with some valuable insights as to how you are doing as a leader, how your team is doing, and how the organization as a whole is performing. You cannot fix something unless you know that it's broken. You cannot improve who you are or anyone else in your department unless you know how you are doing. Focus on each area of your business that interacts with customers and channel your energies into identifying what's working for them, and what's not. Use the information you receive to improve what you are doing so both you and your team can learn together, grow together and be better, together.

Crisis Management

How you've managed crises in the past can teach your team members how to deal with it effectively as a team. Share your previous experiences with them, letting them know that you've been in a similar situation before, and tell them how you handled it. Guaranteed, you would not have gotten it right the first time around. You can probably share several experiences with your team when you've made monumental mistakes.

What's most important here would be what you learned from your mistakes. These should serve as lessons for your team on "what not to do." Crisis management brings intense emotions with it. Share your feelings with the team without allowing any of these emotions to cloud effective leadership.

Diversity Management

Remember when you were first introduced to working with individuals from different backgrounds. While this should never influence the way we lead a group of people, it often does. Accept that everyone is unique, and their individuality should be celebrated rather than having differences highlighted. Differences often make for valuable and unique teams. Differences aren't always physical attributes. They could also be whether or not we encourage inclusion in our teams. As a leader, if you recognize that certain team members are more introverted than others, it's your job to make them feel that what they have to say matters.

Mistakes

Remember mistakes that you've made, or where you've made a poor judgment call and the consequences to those decisions. Use this experience as a reminder to be more considerate in decision-making. Part of the human condition is that we all make mistakes. What's most important, though, is to remember the cost of poor decision-making. This could be a financial cost, a time cost, or even a reputational cost. Poor decision-making will always occur, but it should occur less frequently the longer you're in a leadership position if you're using previous experience as a predictor of future behavior.

No form of failure feels good. Admitting that we've failed is worse. If it's any consolation, every successful leader has a string of failures behind them because it's one of the best ways to be able to learn, grow, and progress. The most important part of failure is learning from it. If we keep making the same mistakes repeatedly, we've learned nothing, and we should go back to the beginning. The best way to learn from failure is to dissect the event, our actions, as well as the outcome or result. Once this has been done, it becomes easier to identify what went wrong so we don't repeat the same mistake again. Sharing what we learned with others is another way of preventing similar mistakes.

Finding Solutions

Tapping into past experiences to make you a better leader is not always negative. Coming up with successful solutions to problems you've encountered in the past can encourage you to be consistent and tenacious in finding solutions for current problems. If you've succeeded in the past, you can do so again in the future.

Dealing With Change

Dealing with change can be disruptive, especially if it's management changes where you've been close to someone for a number of years. Think about previous times when you've had to work through change in the past, and how you managed to do so successfully. It may be worth remembering your first day walking into the organization when you were the bright, shiny, new penny. Leaders complete with their different styles will come and go, and being able to recall how you've dealt with it before willassist your teamwork through it effectively now.

Initiative

Taking initiative can be challenging, especially in an event where it's not encouraged, but it's necessary. Think about times when you were forced to come up with creative solutions towards solving problems. This may make you dig deep and challenge parts of yourself that you are maybe not comfortable with, especially if you have worked in an environment where you were told what you needed to do and when you needed to do it.

Learning New Things

Leadership means being prepared to learn new things and broaden your scope of experience. As we've listed each of the above items, there are probably many more that have sprung to mind. There will be times when you'll be forced to think about situations in the past and make use of them by bringing all this experience together. Experience is something that nobody can ever take away from you. It can either be used to your advantage to make you a better leader, or it can be left to stagnate, which results in having almost no value whatsoever. Experience is something that you're able to pass onto your team.

Expertise

We may not always realize how much valuable knowledge and expertise we have gained over the years that can be applied to everyday work situations. Not all experience needs to come from the workplace. You may have learned something regarding brainstorming or active listening when you were a student. These skills never leave you, and you tap into them on a regular basis. Just because they happen to be used as part of your leadership skills, doesn't mean that you must acquire them in the workplace. Many of these are soft skills, which are "personal attributes that enable someone to interact effectively and harmoniously with other people" (Oxford English Online, 2020).

Some of the most important lessons that you can learn as a leader often come from mistakes that colleagues make. Pay attention to what they do, especially things that either work or don't work. In doing so, you're able to avoid following in their footsteps.

Leading Is Doing

There are several important points to be made when it comes to actually "doing" and leading effectively. Deciding to do the work yourself and taking assignments back from your team will prevent them from learning, growing, making their own decisions, and making their own mistakes. It's important for them to be able to gain this experience for themselves by doing, rather than having a leader who is controlling.

Some leaders become frustrated because they're not necessarily seeing the results that they would like from their team. Instead of using this as a teaching or training experience, they adopt the attitude that it's easier to do the work themselves. Leading from the front means leading by example, while not doing the work. It's being able to encourage and inspire employees to deliver their very best work.

Leading from the front means being prepared to set the best example for your team to follow by respecting your superiors and the chain of command within your organization. It requires an effective delegation and follow-through process once this has been done. It's building your team by fostering relationships of trust. Once you've delegated the work, step back and allow those you lead work with what you've assigned to them.

Employees will mimic leaders when it comes to working habits. It can also be seen in your attitude towards those you lead. Are you genuinely concerned about their well-being and happiness in the workplace? Are they aware that you care enough about them that you'd prefer to see them grow into leaders themselves? This means stepping back and allowing them to fail occasionally. Allowing them to do so gives you the opportunity to mold them into potential leaders themselves, and so the cycle of leadership development begins to take effect.

If you commit to rewarding your team or even individual employees for work completed, such as projects, meeting production targets, or achieving a sales goal, be sure to follow through as promised. This will allow those you lead to recognize you as someone of your word and will earn greater respect from each of them. Remember what you were like before stepping into a leadership role; you may gain some valuable insight as to what your team is currently going through right now.

Chapter 4: Leadership Toughness

"Don't wait until everything is just right. It will never be perfect. There will always be challenges, obstacles and less than perfect conditions. So what? Get started now. With each step you take, you will grow stronger and stronger, more and more skilled, more and more self-confident, and more and more successful."

~ Mark Victor Hansen

Mental Toughness

The pressure is building up, deadlines are hanging over your head, or it's inching closer towards month-end and you still have targets to be met. Management is beginning to apply greater force than you're used to. Your next steps are determined by your degree of mental toughness. Whether you choose to sink or swim depends on whether or not you can persevere, remaining productive during this period. The alternative is to give up and allow the current to drag you down with it. Can mental toughness be taught, and if so, how do you learn it and apply it to your current work environment?

Ask athletes across various sports and almost all of them will tell you that most of their success has come through mental toughness coaching. Once they have successfully developed how to apply mental toughness in any situation, they can consistently do their best despite the circumstances they find themselves in.

For leaders to be successful when faced with challenges, they need to be flexible and display a degree of mental plasticity. This means being prepared to change direction at a moment's notice without digging your heels in. Instead, it's welcoming fresh, new ideas that may present solutions to getting the job done, rather than insisting that the old way is the right way. It's opening your mind to new ideas that may just be better than the old ways.

The acquisition of new skills and knowledge comes with mental toughness because you're prepared to admit that you don't know everything. For business leaders, this is often one of the most difficult admissions to make. So, where should you be turning for this new advice or knowledge? This depends on the situation, but the fact is that the leader is prepared to look for new answers to new problems. Because we're faced with brand new challenges daily, we need to continue searching for innovative solutions. Gaining the required knowledge may mean re-learning skills that we've forgotten.

Part of successful business leadership is continuous growth and learning results in growth, helping teams and organizations move forward towards their ultimate goals. Learning should be a life-long event, and as a leader, you can hand this ambition to those reporting to you.

Resilience is at the very heart of mental toughness, as this provides the flexibility to bounce back, especially in the event of failure (which happens to all of us). It's being able to get up every single time you get knocked down or defeated, no matter what. Resilience is a choice that you make and how you plan to face change whenever it's presented to you. It's your mental, emotional, and physical response to defeat, or other obstacles that happen to be placed in front of you. Resilience is looking for opportunities where you can learn and grow from a situation, rather than blaming others.

Response time can be a major contributing factor to mental toughness. Those who sit around and wait, or mull back and forth over ideas before deciding can impact the overall outcome. With mental toughness, it's important that you come up with a solution as quickly as possible. Even if it's not the right decision, it gives you a platform to continue searching for solutions from. Wasting time is a valuable commodity that most businesses don't have the luxury of doing, especially in the competitive world in which we're currently living. Those who can make rapid decisions to resolve problems can remain one step ahead of their opposition.

Mentally tough leaders have a strength that runs deeper than their ability to remain mentally and physically alert and responsive during challenging times. These strengths give them the tenacity to see each challenge through to the end no matter what. It's the ability to remain focused on whether you win or lose. Mental toughness should be a skill that every successful leader acquires. According to Leadership Strategist, Tony Ewing, there are certain things that leaders with emotional toughness never do (Ewing, 2020):

• They never make important decisions when they're feeling emotional. Scientifically, it's been proven that cognitive control affects the decision-making process, and this is influenced by our emotions. As a result, any major decisions should rather be made when you're feeling both rational and clear-headed. (Inzlicht et al., 2015).

• Those who are mentally tough don't delay making decisions. They don't need to waste time trying to come up with the right solution to the problem. They consider all the facts available and decide on what their intuition tells them will be best for all parties concerned.

• They don't jump to conclusions without background information. Those who are mentally tough ensure they have as many facts, figures, and information available to them as possible. They identify when insufficient information is available to make a decision, and will remove themselves from the decision-making process. They don't need the information to support their conclusion. They consider the pros and cons of the given situation and decide based on the information available.

• They don't need the approval of others as part of their decision-making process. They're not swayed by having to be popular or not.

• They accept reality and don't assume they can never be wrong. They operate from a viewpoint of reality where everyone is a part. They don't separate themselves from everyone else with a different viewpoint.

• They don't avoid change; instead, they embrace it as change means growth (Ewing, 2020).

When Leaders Are at Their Best

As part of this section, we are going to be looking at several ways where you can benchmark your own performance as a leader by asking yourself several key questions and being brutally honest with the answers. It's only once you do this that you can be certain whether you're at your best as a leader.

Are Your Team Members Thriving or Stagnating?

One of the most important questions to ask yourself as a benchmark for successful leadership is to assess whether the individuals reporting to you are thriving or stagnating. You need to monitor them often by spending time with them individually, following up on work they've been assigned to do, and conducting regular feedback interviews or meetings with them. Employing EQ skills will help you assess the body language of the team. This will allow you to gain a better perspective on how they feel towards you as their leader, and towards their work. Mastering emotional intelligence skills will benefit you throughout your career, and not just while leading your current team.

By getting to know each member of your team individually, they will open up and share their hopes and dreams with you, as well as their goals for the future. To lead them successfully, you need this information (even though it may seem unimportant at the time). By truly connecting with them on such a personal level, you will not only have things to discuss that are outside the realm of "work," but you will display a genuine concern for those you lead, rather than a superficial relationship where you get the corner office and have minimal communication with your team. The ability to connect personally will allow you to encourage the achievement of their goals, whether personal or professional.

Do your team members know what your top priorities for the year are? If not, why not? As the leader of a team that has shared visions and goals to be working towards, it should be automatically "given" that your goals and priorities are closely aligned with those of the organization, and that your team knows exactly what these are. Similarly, getting to know those for which you're responsible will help you to gain a better understanding of their hopes and dreams and career aspirations. Don't be afraid of letting your team members get close enough to you to know exactly where you want to be in both the short- and long-term. Too many leaders assume the leadership role should separate them from their team. Successful leaders work collaboratively and collectively with those under them. They have their sights set on a common goal, and aren't afraid to share this knowledge with others that can assist them in their quest.

Do your team members feel that they can come to you with anything, or are they afraid of you as a leader, especially when it comes to failing? Let's face it; none of us likes to fail. It makes us feel horrible, and we begin to question our abilities, and get all hung-up in self-loathing, pity, blame, and all those other self-defeating thoughts and emotions. If you are the best you can be as a leader, this team member won't be afraid of failure because they would know that it presents an opportunity for them to learn and grow, and that even you, as their leader, have failed from time to time.

Working with a team that is functioning out of fear, rather than loyalty and passion, won't produce the best results. You will constantly have them second-guessing themselves and one another, as well as your ability to lead from the front in an ever-changing world of work. Ideally, they are looking for a leader that is both accountable and responsible for those they lead. These two words hold such importance for organizations and teams alike because so many leaders aren't prepared to accept accountability or responsibility for those they manage.

It's become far easier to point fingers in the direction of others, rather than accepting accountability, looking for solutions that can be applied to the problem and acting responsibly. These are the characteristics of a true leader. Someone who's not afraid of failing, and instead recognizes failure as part of leadership and a way to further develop his or her leadership skills.

Successful leaders are open to new ideas and welcome these from members of their team. They realize that they don't know everything that there is to know on every subject. This would be an impossible feat, however, by looking towards those of their team who possess increased knowledge in certain areas, so they're sure to receive the right input. This is especially effective when working closely to brainstorm, come up with fresh new ideas, or overcome a specific problem or challenge that you may be facing at the time.

Excellent leaders are more focused on passing on the positive skills they have learned as a leader as a means of creating more leaders or successors. The thought of coaching or mentoring others into leadership roles doesn't threaten them because they understand that part of the growth process will mean learning to let go and move on at some stage. What better legacy to be able to leave behind than someone who has developed strong leadership attributes at the side of an effective leader?

Successful leaders are empathetic and kind. They aren't judgmental, and accept that people are human and are subject to many things in life. They aren't afraid of showing this "softer" side of their personality because they don't believe that it makes them weak. Instead, they recognize that it makes them more human for those they lead.

True leaders are flexible in their leadership style. They are prepared to shift into different management modes, depending on what each situation calls for. These leaders can also adjust their management style to suit the individuals under them. In some instances, team members can work on their own, totally unsupervised, and unmanaged, while others need to be micromanaged and their work needs to be checked several times to ensure that it's correct before anything can be done with it. It's being able to successfully morph between the two, without losing credibility with your team. Ideally, these shifts would be so subtle that your team hardly even notices the difference.

Successful managers constantly provide direct feedback on individual performance. This is done regularly and privately so that individuals who need firmer encouragement aren't embarrassed in front of their colleagues. This is a characteristic that will always hold you in good stead and you should reward your team members openly with any awards or recognition, and chastise those who need correction or redirection in private. Nobody benefits from public humiliation; all that happens is the leader loses credibility in the eyes of the team.

Great leaders manage to keep a positive attitude, no matter what's going on around them—this, in turn, keeps the team productive and motivated. These leaders can successfully hide when things are going sideways or if they're facing a personal crisis. All that's important is ensuring that bottom-line results are achieved, and achieved consistently. Leaders encourage those reporting to them to constantly be bottom-line conscious in all that they do. It's easy for employees to get caught up in the work environment that they don't see the business operating costs as part of the organization. Great leaders can point these out to their employees in such a way that they are prepared to collaborate towards trimming these unseen expenses.

Excellent leaders are prepared to step out of their comfort zone and do uncomfortable things. Some of these may be making tough decisions that affect the business organization (such as hiring or firing). Whatever it is, when times are uncomfortable and the pressure is on, mental toughness, as discussed previously, as well as being strong enough emotionally to make difficult decisions, becomes apparent.

Great leaders are results-centric. This means that they're all about producing results, no matter what it takes. Whether these are production results, sales results, customer service indices, whatever they may be, true leaders understand that without a marketplace, there would be no business organization, and they protect it at all costs. They also make it their business to understand all areas of the business operation, so they remain informed and up-to-date with any and all aspects of the organization.

Excellent leaders have clear employee goals and expectations. Because they know each of their employees, they know what to expect from them, how far they can push them, and whether their employees are coping successfully or not.

Great leaders are prepared to teach their employees how things should be done instead of giving orders and expecting employees to understand. They don't expect employees to do anything that they cannot do themselves (unless the employee is a specialist and has been hired for this purpose).

As leaders, their vision is clearly defined, and they understand their own motivation. They willingly share this information with those on their team to inspire and motivate others to follow.

Leaders are humble yet curious creatures. They give credit where credit is due, but are willing to take the fall for their team whenever necessary. They seldom think of themselves first, instead; it's about the organization and the team, rather than the leader.

Chapter 5: Extraordinary Leadership

"Always dream and shoot higher than you know you can do. Don't bother just to be better than your contemporaries or predecessors. Try to do better than yourself."

~ William Faulkner

Making Extraordinary Things Happen

Discovering how to hone your talents and skills as an extraordinary leader means being able to roll up your sleeves and getting into the trenches with your staff. Having interviewed numerous successful, forward-thinking CEOs, performance strategist and author of *The Genius Habit*, Laura Garnett has identified the following as key elements in your leadership strategy of moving from good to great (Garnett, 2015):

Allow Others to Lead

It's difficult allowing those you lead to take the reins for a while for them to learn and grow, not only as individuals, but maybe as part of their career aspirations. As their leader, you should know to whom you can entrust this within your group. Maybe you'd like to rotate the leadership responsibility with each team member, allowing them to discover for themselves what leadership skills they possess. You may find some individuals who will automatically shrink backward at this opportunity. Don't force them or make them feel even more uncomfortable by calling them out. Not everyone is born to lead. There are many who are quite comfortable following and doing what is required of them. As their leader, you should know who these individuals are already. Assign them some other tasks that are better suited to who they are.

Ask Critical Questions

Asking the right questions at the right time will provide valuable insights into the team and how it progresses as a cohesive unit. Asking the right questions allows you to put those you lead first. It can remove you from being too close to a situation (allowing you to see things from a different perspective) to come up with creative solutions. Asking questions will help you understand your team better as well as gaining a clearer knowledge of their hopes and aspirations for the future.

Focus on Diversity and Overcoming Bias

Extraordinary leaders respect the thoughts and opinions of those they lead. They don't assume that their way of thinking is always correct. Because of this, they are open to new thoughts, suggestions, and innovative ideas from those they manage. They embrace the diversity of thought, recognizing that we are each unique and don't need to think the same way to be extraordinary. According to Timothy Wilson, a psychology professor at the University of Virginia and author of *Strangers to Ourselves: Discovering the Adaptive Unconscious*, the brain, is bombarded by an average of 11 million pieces of information at any given moment. Wilson confirms that because we are only able to process around 40 pieces of this information, the brain creates shortcuts and works from historical data and past experiences to make present assumptions. As leaders, we often settle for the first answer to a problem, purely because it falls into one of these 40 suppositions. This doesn't mean that better answers aren't out there, and we should be challenging ourselves to find them (Porter, 2014).

Lead by Example

One of the most important elements of leadership is doing what you expect others to do and leading through your own example. Members of your team will be quick to follow whatever you do. They look to you as a source of inspiration and guidance. If your example is one of egocentric behavior, that's exactly what you're going to get out of your team. On the other hand, if you are passionate about your work, you have a strong moral code and work ethic, you're reliable and dependable, then this is exactly what your team will present to you.

Much of what your team members do will be a mirror-image to your behavior. If there's something there that you don't like, or happens to be disrupting the functionality of the team, it may be time to look inwards and examine your own work ethics.

Play to The Strengths of Your Team

As a leader over a team, it's your job to understand each team member thoroughly. This means knowing what their hopes, dreams, and aspirations for the future are. Where do they see themselves in a year from now? Five years from now, and so on. Are they looking to someday take over for you, being able to manage their own team, or do they have greater aspirations that have nothing to do with their current position? By knowing and understanding your team, you should know exactly what their strengths and limitations are. What do they want to accomplish over the short-term? How can you, as their leader assist them to reach this goal?

As you work with your team, allow each of them to play towards their strengths. If someone is great at negotiations, place them in a position where this skill can be used to its maximum capacity. Others don't necessarily like the limelight. Perhaps they prefer working in the background crunching numbers. That's okay, there's a place for these individuals. Don't force them into the foreground to see whether they can handle pressure—you already know the answer. They may well be able to handle extreme pressure when it comes to numbers and deadlines. Give them the opportunity to shine, doing what they're best at doing. If you stick to this recipe, your business will succeed all the time.

Reignite Your Own Leadership Flame

We are all entitled to have bad days when things don't seem to go right, and we question our own ability to lead others. Remember that you are also only human, and because of this, you need to arm yourself with those skills and attributes that will help you to pull yourself out to these ruts whenever they appear. Learn to recognize the signs for whenever you feel yourself being pulled off your game. Set a game plan for whenever this happens to help reignite your leadership flame. Only you will know what works for you. For some, it takes quiet introspection, analyzing and diagnosing whatever has gone wrong and trying to come up with creative ways to fix these mistakes. For others, it's being able to use a mentor or trusted friend as a sounding board to bounce ideas around. Others like to discuss this with their team, allowing them to peek behind the curtain briefly to see that you are still only human after all.

One important takeaway from this section is that we all face downtimes as leaders. This will always be the case. What's important is to try and recognize what sets these lows off and how to deal with each of them effectively. Knowing this will assist you to snap out of it much quicker the next time it occurs. Being aware of yourself, your emotions, and your way of thinking to display high emotional intelligence, a characteristic that you want to develop and be able to share with those you lead (Garnett, 2015).

The Practices of Excellent Leadership

In this section, we are going to focus our attention on some of the world's greatest leaders, considering what has made them great, what sets them apart, and what they are possibly doing differently than other leaders in a rapidly changing world.

Jeff Bezos, Founder, and CEO of Amazon

Further to a statement made by Jeff Bezos to the U.S. House of Representatives at the end of July 2020, Bezos tells his own story about how he created Amazon out of his garage some 26 years ago. His childhood was not the easiest, his mother became pregnant as a teenager, and it was only thanks to the tenacity of his grandfather that she could continue with her classes. Moving onto college, she went to night school, taking classes that would allow her to take her small child along with her.

Jeff was adopted by Miguel, a Cuban immigrant who was sent to America in search of the "American Dream," by his parents shortly after Castro took over. Having obtained a scholarship to study, he met Jeff's mom, Jackie, as they attended the same college. Miguel and Jackie married, and Jeff was adopted at the age of four. Between this time and when Jeff was 16, he was fortunate enough to spend most of his summers on his grandparents' ranch in Texas. There, he was taught the value of hard work. He learned that you couldn't just rely on someone coming out to repair things as they broke. With the ranch situated in the middle of nowhere, Jeff watched his grandfather come up with innovative solutions to solve problems that often looked as though they were impossible.

The lessons Jeff learned from his grandfather spurred him onto attempting his own inventions as a teenager.

By 1994, Jeff had visualized Amazon. Creating an online bookstore with millions of books appealed to him. It was impossible at the time. Although he was already working full-time at an investment company in New York, he could not help but answer the call of destiny pulling him towards his dream. His manager tried to convince him to stay once he had decided to resign, by encouraging him to think about it, rather than jumping in blindly. The answer Jeff gave him two days later was that he would rather attempt his dream and fail, than live a life not knowing what would have happened had he been given the opportunity.

Jeff began Amazon out of his garage with the financial backing of his parents. At the time, the Internet was still in its infancy, and they never even grasped the concept of this "online bookstore" that he had envisioned. Jeff was honest with them and told them that there was about a 70% chance that they were likely to lose their entire investment. They backed him anyway. Another 50 meetings later, Jeff had managed to raise $1 million as startup capital for his business.

Initially, Jeff drove packages to be posted himself, dreaming of days when the business could expand. By 2001, the business was almost $3 billion in debt. Between the start of the business and the fourth quarter of 2001, the press had a field day with Amazon as a brand, constantly punting it as a failure. Looking back, Bezos will be the first to admit that billions were spent on failures, and that failures come as a result of risk-taking. He also admits that in order to become successful, you must be able to fail and learn something from each of those lessons. According to him, Amazon is the best place to learn to fail.

Two words regarding their business align with his original vision for the business, and that's "Day One." By encouraging everyone within the organization to have a Day One approach to the business, they would simply not have a "failure" mentality.

The main vision of Amazon was to create an organization that was customer-centric. A place where people would keep coming back because of their customer experience. It was never about the product or the books; it was about providing the best possible service available over an e-commerce site (before e-commerce sites were all that popular).

He admits that customer service is something that's challenging to win over and to manage to hold onto, but this has always been the main vision behind the Amazon brand. It was and is, putting the customer first, every single time. Putting the customer first meant innovating ahead of customer needs, and not waiting for them to recommend or ask for additional services to be added into the mix. Amazon managed to do this all on its own, and introduced its Prime membership program. They have also been actively working on speeding up warehousing and delivery times by growing nationally and internationally.

In the early days, Bezos admits that there were threats that Amazon would be swallowed up by other publishing giants, such as Barnes and Noble. Of course, they never felt threatened by Amazon and left him alone. Today, there are many things that set Amazon apart from the rest and it's these things that are the takeaway from his style of leadership:

- Trust is earned slowly

- Do hard things well

- Deliver on time

- Keep promises

- Make tough decisions

- Give customers back time

These are key factors that Bezos has always held at the heart of Amazon. Right now, he shares the spotlight with Elon Musk as the number one ranked business leader in the United States. For him though, it's still about keeping the "Day One" mentality, and this is promoted throughout the organization. The vision he had for Amazon when there were 10 employees, when there were 10,000 employees, 100,000 employees is the same.

As a business, Amazon gives back. Bezos believes in education, in advancing and providing opportunities for those who have been previously disadvantaged. As an organization, they are fully invested in reducing the carbon footprint by ordering 100,000 electric vehicles to be fully operational by 2030. They have invested billions of dollars in their career program, that isn't just limited to studies that will benefit Amazon. Bezos believes that you need to be able to follow your passion. He fully supports the "garage entrepreneurial" spirit, but adds that thanks to the current scale of Amazon, there's so much more that he can do to make a difference and give back. From solar and wind energy, to employing 175,000 new employees over a two-month period during the recent pandemic. The list of ways that Amazon is giving back to the world is almost endless, all because one young man had the vision to bring unprecedented customer service experience to the consumer, ensuring customer loyalty (Bezos, 2020).

Chapter 6: Leadership Qualities / Values

"The challenge of leadership is to be strong, but not rude; be kind, but not weak; be bold, but not bully; be thoughtful, but not lazy; be humble, but not timid; be proud, but not arrogant; have humor, but without folly."

~ Jim Rohn

Leadership Studies

Studies conducted by leadership expert training organization, "Dale Carnegie Training," indicated that, often, expectations that employees have regarding their leaders fall way short.

They specifically list five key areas that need leadership improvement. This study was conducted using more than 3,300 employees globally, with 515 coming from the United States. The study revealed that 84% of workers wanted their leaders to take accountability when they made mistakes, while only 51% of leaders were currently doing so. 88% wanted leaders to really listen to them, while only 61% confirmed that they had leaders who took communication, especially the active listening component of communication, seriously. 86% of those surveyed wanted leaders to recognize them for good work. Only 60% confirmed that this was taking place.

The author of the study wrote that "Employees want leaders who develop themselves and others, making it safe to share their ideas, try new things, make mistakes, learn from them and improve" (Business News Daily Expert Editor, 2016).

Another survey was completed using 5,000 individuals by The Predictive Index to define "what makes a great boss." This indicated that humility, passion, patience, and self-awareness, were the top five skills that most individuals surveyed identified as key characteristics. These traits were necessary for individuals to flourish rather than just get by (Koch, 2019).

The five key attributes that employees were looking for in the Dale Carnegie Training study as reported in Business News Daily, were the following:

Accountability

To be accountable is for leaders to recognize that they are not perfect and have their own set of faults that needed to be managed or overcome, rather than criticizing employees for getting things wrong. 68% of employees were motivated if their leaders indicated that they were also only human and made mistakes from time to time. The ideal way to deal with mistakes as an employee or a leader is to acknowledge that the fault is there, to begin with, to own up to it immediately when a mistake is made (rather than trying to ignore it in the hope that the error will disappear). The next step would be to correct whatever has gone wrong as quickly as possible by coming up with a suitable solution. Often, this means communicating about it and brainstorming suitable solutions to find the best one. For employees, just getting this right was one way that made their leaders more approachable.

Providing Encouragement

This is like the above, yet the shoe is on the other foot and the employee happens to be the one who has made the mistake. 60% of employees would prefer it if their leader gave them the opportunity to correct whatever has been done incorrectly. We've already discussed how important it is to correct someone in private and reward them openly. There's nothing that damages an employer/employee relationship like reprimanding them openly for errors that anyone could have made.

Offering encouragement by recognizing that your employee has improved in an area of their work will take only a moment to do, but can make all the difference in the life of that employee. More than 70% of employees recognized that this should be a vital characteristic for leaders to master to gain respect. As a leader, cast your mind back to when you just started out in the big scary world of work. There were probably many things that you needed to learn before you could really claim competence. This is the same scenario. Your employees don't need to be perfect at something just yet to qualify for encouragement. Recognize that there has been improvement in their work, no matter how small it may seem to you. You will find that your employees will give you a lot more when they are feeling content and happy.

Recognition and Reward

Small tokens of praise and appreciation would go a long way to keep employees motivated and encouraged to give of their best. 75% of leaders miss the boat when it comes to offering their teams small tokens of appreciation or recognition and rewards for doing things well. A large international call center for which I consulted in 2013 used this extremely effectively by gathering their 300+ workforce each Monday morning. The CEO and executive management team would have identified several individuals across the various divisions. They would then be recognized in front of the entire organization. Some of these awards were certificates, cash incentives, or vouchers, product hampers, or promotions within the organization. As a management team, these leaders understood what it meant to keep staff motivated and working towards internal goals and incentives.

On-the-job-Coaching/Training

True leaders arrange for their employees to receive constant encouragement to help them improve within their work. As many as 80% of those surveyed indicated that the best leaders provided learning opportunities for them to develop and grow within the workplace. This doesn't always need to be internal training, coaching, or mentoring. This could also include sending your employees for job-specific training that doesn't only benefit them, but it will benefit the entire organization. It's providing the employee with the best opportunity to be the very best they could be at their job.

The results for leaders who are willing to embrace each of these methods could be extremely positive, not only for themselves as the business leader, but also as far as retention strategies are concerned. Happy employees want to stay and grow within organizations, rather than seeking these qualities from other leaders out there.

Respect from those to whom they report is a major factor, where those who felt as though their leaders respected them, 55% were more engaged in their work than those who never felt secure. Respecting others is more than just saying that you respect them— it's an action. Knowing what your weaknesses through self-awareness make you a better leader.

Honesty/Integrity

Honesty and integrity go hand-in-hand when it comes to leadership and what's required by the workforce to feel as though they can trust you. Employees are quick to pick up on half-truths and (or) lies. It's better to always be honest , rather than bringing up things that are not honest. Part of this is admitting when you're wrong.

Accountability and responsibility may not always be pleasant, but they will help you gain the respect of those you work with and those reporting to you. It's often the little things that we think we can get away with. We tell a little white lie here, and then a little white lie there, feeling confident that each of the lies are small, and there's harm that can come from these small untruths. The problem with lying is that small lies turn into bigger lies, and eventually the lines get so blurred that there's no distinct difference between what's real and what's not.

A leader should be able to stand by whatever they've said and whenever they've said it, because the truth will always remain the same. A lie, on the other hand, is not designed for longevity as the brain is not wired for us to default to an untruth. That's one of the reasons why body language can allow you to easily tell when someone is lying or not. The mind will sift through millions and millions of pieces of information that's stored in your mental mainframe to try and "recall" exactly what you said. There will always be small differences between stories, and when these are each tallied, the lie(s) become easily exposed.

Credibility

Developing credibility as a leader doesn't happen automatically, or overnight. Instead, it takes a fair amount of time for employees to get to know their leaders sufficiently enough to be able to trust them. According to Peter Economy, leadership specialist at Inc., only 49% of employees trust executive leadership. This statistic is high when you consider how many employees feel as though they cannot trust those who lead them daily. What determines whether a leader is credible or not? There are certain characteristics that credible leaders all share. They practice these leadership qualities daily, and this is what sets them apart (Economy, 2015):

- They accept accountability for actions and decisions

- They are experts in their field and can assist coming up with solid working solutions to problems

- They are loyal and display a genuine concern for others

- They are transparent and open and honest in all things

- They can delegate effectively, which builds up trust from those they lead

- They have a strong moral code and align with their ethics

- They look for win-win solutions for all

- They respect others and that respect is reciprocal in return

- They understand that to be able to lead, they need to learn, and that learning is life-long

- They walk-the-walk and talk-the-talk

Motivation

It's one thing being able to motivate yourself and keep yourself going throughout the day, but consistently motivating those reporting to you is something different. Considering this characteristic from the employees' perspective, this is what they need from you as their leader:

- A popular way of becoming motivated in the business through team building events that can boost morale.
- Gaining a perspective from the employee's point of view as another way to motivate them through understanding.
- Involving employees in the decision-making process by teaching them specific areas of the business, motivating them through being taught how the business operates.

Motivation could come from being able to influence individuals towards your way of thinking. It's also helping employees achieve their goals, assisting with personal development in the process.

Motivation is the key to boosting the achievement of personal development goals within an organization that has been identified by the employee.

Rewards and recognition, as we spoke about earlier, could be a way to motivate certain employees, if the rewards are aligned with something the employee feels will be beneficial. Often, this can be as small as a letter of thanks for the work completed. These should be genuine and heartfelt to be effective.

Successful motivation means understanding those reporting to you and what they specifically need individually. One person's needs may be completely different from that of another, and it's your job as a leader to ensure that you can align all these needs with those of the organization.

You can motivate by setting the right example for employees to follow by being an effective role model for them to follow.

Serving

These leaders place their employees first. They understand that being able to collaborate and encourage their team to produce the very best is possible. Results are based on empowerment and upliftment rather than being told what to do all the time. Servant leaders spend time unlocking the creativity and individual potential that may be trapped inside each employee, just waiting to find its way to the surface. This leadership style is where the magic happens, and where employees become more productive because they feel more invested in the organization. Serving is all about the employee, rather than the employer or the leader in the employer's organization.

Awareness

Awareness in leadership could be actual awareness of those who report to them, or awareness of themselves as leaders. Self-awareness is a vital emotional intelligence skill that needs to be tapped into for effective leadership. Authors of *Emotional Intelligence 2.0*, Travis Bradberry and Jean Greaves, state that "83% of people with high self-awareness are top performers ..." (Bradberry & Greaves, 2009).

There are several ways you can boost your self-awareness:

• Are you living true to your belief system, or have you lost your way somehow, getting derailed by the speed at which we live our lives now? Do you feel good about the choices, decisions, and ultimately the path that you're headed towards now? Therefore, self-awareness is so important in leadership. You need to be able to see what's happening in your own life before being able to make changes in the lives of others.

• Ask those you trust for feedback; this might provide some insight into your emotions. Get this feedback from various places, like from colleagues, friends, family members—the broader the input, the more likely you are to get insight that's worthwhile. Having to endure feedback (especially when negative) may be a painful experience, however, it's this feedback that has the greatest value. The feedback received can allow you to see how you communicate with other people.

• Be open to change and adapt along with your team. A great example of this is if you feel most productive towards the end of the day so you always insist on having strategic team meetings during that time. Have you stopped to consider when others are most productive? Have you ever asked? It may mean shifting things around and scheduling these meetings shortly before lunch. You may suddenly receive optimal input from those in your team because you've been prepared to negotiate to meet their needs rather than those of your own.

• Becoming more aware of your feelings, what they mean, and how they're influencing you in the workplace. When you cannot control your own emotions, it's impossible to try and understand the emotions of your team. The best thing to do is to allow your feelings to run their course without holding onto them. Pay attention to the emotions and what they may be trying to teach you. In most instances, there are lessons to be learned from our feelings.

• Get to know yourself better by keeping track of your moods, emotions, and mental and physical states. Keep a journal nearby so that you can write these down. Keep making regular notes without passing judgment or making changes for a couple of months. From there, you will be in a much better place to begin to identify triggers or patterns that cause you to do the things you do. You can also begin to make changes, still tracking each of these in your journal. It's often a healthier sounding board to write your thoughts and emotions down rather than physically lashing out at staff or even at home. It's a great way to recognize personal growth within yourself and coming to terms with areas that need personal growth.

• What are your strengths and weaknesses? Have you asked for feedback from others on this? What you perceive to be strengths or weaknesses may be viewed by others as completely different, especially those under you. Make a list of the feedback you receive so you have a starting point to either further develop (your strengths) or be aware of, as a means of making necessary changes.

• What messages is your body language sending out there? What can you do to change it from being closed and negative, to more open and positive?

Empathy

Empathy is at the very center of being an effective leader. It proves that you have the capacity to be concerned about those you lead. According to Lolly Daskal, author of *The Leadership Gap: What Gets Between You and Your Greatness*, you can use the following ways to improve your skills as an empathetic leader:

• Connect with those you lead by attempting to understanding them better

• Empathy is a core skill necessary for effective leadership

• Empathy strengthens your ability to communicate successfully

- Learn to be more patient with your team

- Pay close attention to those you lead by being in the moment

- Put yourself in their situation before judging them or jumping to conclusions

Empathy is another emotional intelligence skill that can be acquired through extensive practice. It's being able to read the body language and cues that your team are transmitting. Empathy means that you can place yourself in the shoes of those of your team, while seeing things from their perspective rather than your own. It's a humanizing element in leadership. You can show you care about those you lead, without looking soft (Daskal, 2016).

Creativity

Creativity and leadership appear to be at opposite ends of another, however, this has become more and more important for business success. Examples of creative geniuses include individuals such as Steve Jobs, who had a brand-new vision for Apple, Elon Musk, Richard Branson, Mary Barra, and Mark Zuckerberg.

Elon Musk has been prepared to face bankruptcy to get SpaceX off the ground, despite being mocked and ridiculed from those within and outside of his own organization.

Richard Branson has always been about his employees, taking care of them and listening to them. He understands that without his people, there would not be a multi-billion- dollar organization behind the Virgin brand.

Following several deaths due to ignition failures in some of their models, General Motors' newly appointed CEO and Chairman, Mary Barra, decided to make the biggest recall decision in the history of GM. While she knew that this wasn't likely to score her any popularity points with the GM Board, she also knew it was the right thing to do. This single decision has made her one of the most recognized CEOs in the world today.

Finally, but by no means a lightweight in the creativity department, Mark Zuckerberg only hires on passion rather than skill. It's his belief that skill can be taught, yet passion needs to be part of who the individual is.

Each of these leaders has found creative ways to work through some of their toughest problems. Being prepared to put creativity into action and allowing your employees to come up with creative solutions that your organization may be facing right now. Don't stifle their ideas; they may just surprise you if they're allowed to innovate and think for themselves.

Thoroughness

Being thorough in your work as a leader covers more than just covering certain areas of your job necessary in a monthly or quarterly report. It comes down to having complete knowledge and understanding of all areas of the business. It's knowing exactly what is required of a specific project or goal being managed by the team. In-depth knowledge means that you can break the task down into manageable components which can be delegated to team members, so that targets are met in line with the organization's requirements. Even though delegation takes place, communication of the entire project has also taken place so that everyone is on board with the program.

Taking Risks

Dr. Sharon Porter, CEO of Perfect Time, founder of The GRIND Entrepreneur Network and *Write the Book Now!* explains why taking risks is important for leaders to become successful. She notes that in her early years of teaching, she was fascinated with the autobiographies of successful leaders, and one of the things that she discovered was that there was no specific formula to becoming a great leader. Instead, there were several ways that one could get there. She recalled advice she'd been given once that she claims to be the best single piece advice ever received: "Don't be afraid to take risks" (S H Porter, 2018).

In truth, this is often an area in leadership where we shy away. We look at taking the safe way because taking risks has the element of potential failure attached to it. Part of taking risks should follow a process of getting used to the size of the risks and making certain that they're calculated. Ensure that you have all the information necessary before jumping in brazenly. Much of the time, this means being in tune with your intuition and listening to what it is telling you.

If you're prepared to take risks, you must be prepared to fail forward and ensure that you are able to dissect the results, and discover what went wrong and what you need to change in order to succeed in the future. Taking risks is often going to lead to failure, so you need to be prepared for it. Many leaders take a risk, fail, and then refuse to ever take another risk again because failure feels uncomfortable (which it should). We should always analyze our failures to discover exactly what went wrong and how things might be changed.

Improving

There are several ways that leaders can focus on improving their own leadership skills in such a way that they not only benefit the team, but positively impact the entire organization. Some of these ways are:

Enroll in Leadership Training: There are many leadership training programs available that are often industry-specific. If there are areas you feel you need to improve on, speak with your direct report, or HR, to find out whether or not the organization is prepared to send you for these training courses. If they say no, it's still worthwhile to invest in yourself and do coursework online or after hours. As the market changes, there are more and more reputable organizations offering online courses that can be completed in your own time. Not only will this assist you in the workplace, but it will be another qualification to add to your current portfolio.

Following Those Leaders You Admire: You can follow business leaders who are currently alive online, or study biographies of those reputable leaders who have died. Several leaders immediately spring to mind, such as Steve Jobs, Nelson Mandela, and Stephen Covey. Each of these leaders had different styles, yet were able to get those who followed them to do remarkable things.

Grow Your Network: Business networking is always a great way of improving your own skills. This is simply being able to move in the same circles as great, effective, and successful business leaders. You may be thinking to yourself that you're on the opposite end of the globe from these people; how could you ever make this work? Quite simply, through social networking. Find them on LinkedIn and make sure that you follow their posts, and engage with them in ways that are worthwhile and meaningful. Facebook is a more sociable platform than LinkedIn, so if you want to be taken seriously, ensure that your communications are always professional and applicable.

Remain Transparent: Allow your team to be aware of what you're all about and what you're doing. This goes a long way to garner respect from them, and as you strive to make improvements in your life, they may become motivated to do the same.

Innovation

Innovation and strategic planning go hand-in-hand. Because the world is changing at an ever-increasing pace, companies need to remain innovative and in front of their competitors. Leaders need to remain ahead of trends and changes in the marketplace. This means tracking what is happening or keeping abreast of changes as they're taking place, rather than burying your head in the sand and pretending that all is well. It's knowing that what has worked in the past may not be good enough for the future and admitting that innovative change is necessary to keep ahead of the pack.

As a leader, this could mean being a catalyst for innovative change through teams coming together with solutions that could be implemented to resolve problems. Innovation is more than just coming up with a good idea. It's being able to see the idea through to a result, without becoming distracted. It's also finding workable solutions when problems arise. Most of this is done by collaborating as a team, rather than just leaving it to a single individual.

Chapter 7: Leadership Skills

"The most dangerous leadership myth is that leaders are born-that there is a genetic factor to leadership. That's nonsense; in fact, the opposite is true. Leaders are made rather than born."

~ Warren Bennis

Leaders: Born or Made?

Whether leaders are naturally born to lead, or whether they can learn how to lead is one of the most asked questions about leadership skills. To answer this conundrum, most refer to it as a similar theory as the chicken and the egg, or nature versus nurture. Unpacking this question a bit further, if you are fortunate enough to be born with innate abilities to lead, then it means that conversely, if you weren't fortunate enough to have hit the gene pool jackpot, you're doomed to sit on the sidelines for the rest of your life.

When being asked the same question, career contributor, Erika Anderson from Forbes shares what she's learned through observing thousands of individuals in business over a 30-year period. She indicates that leadership ability can be compared with a bell curve. Some individuals are born with natural leadership abilities. They would find themselves towards the top of the curve. From here, there's only one way for them and that's upwards towards greater leadership. The 10-15% of individuals towards the bottom of the curve would never make effective leaders no matter how many leadership training courses they attend, or how many leadership books they read. Most of these individuals are quite comfortable with who they are and don't aspire to be leaders.

Between these two opposite ends of the spectrum is the largest area of the curve. These individuals have some natural abilities that they are born with, but most of their leadership abilities are learned.

Career and life coach, Erika Anderson, specifies that leaders who are the easiest to coach, train, re-train, and work with are those who are able to place themselves under the microscope and answer the following questions openly and honestly; while we've spoken of strengths and weaknesses in a number of places already, the secret is being able to answer and identify these in your personal life, as well as from a leadership perspective. She suggests asking yourself the following four questions (it will be worthwhile finding a journal that you can reflect in, to use as a benchmark to monitor your growth and development.)

- Are the things you do in line with the commitments you make to others?

- What things are most important to you in your life?

- Do the things you say and do have an impact on those around you? Is this impact a positive or negative one?

- What direction is your moral compass pointing you towards?

Ensure that you check yourself against these four questions regularly to make certain that you are constantly stretching yourself as a leader. With an ever-changing work environment, you may need to reinvent yourself several times throughout your career (Andersen, 2012).

What People Look for In A Leader

While we've already mentioned a lot of qualities that great leaders possess, there are still several people skills and/or characteristics that employees look for in their leaders. Some of these include, but aren't limited to:

Being Effective at Problem-solving

Displaying effective problem-solving abilities means being in a position where you, as a leader, can recognize problems before they arise. The next step would be to manage each problem effectively before it has the chance to do any real damage. Leaders who demonstrate this ability set positive examples for employees so they can identify resources necessary to find solutions.

Creating an Environment That Doesn't Judge Failure

Let's face it, we all fail as we strive to come up with the best possible solutions to challenges. It may mean that you missed a deadline for submitting a report. Failing feels bad enough, and we tend to judge ourselves more harshly than anyone else ever could. When leaders make certain that the environment is a safe space for failure, employees will be motivated to take more calculated risks, learning as they go.

Providing Mentorship and Training

Great leaders learn to recognize the potential in those they lead early on, and are prepared to do something about it. Remember the example of Amazon, with their study fund for employees. The thing that Bezos got right was not limiting further education and not training purely to things that were of benefit to Amazon. Instead, he encouraged employees to follow their dreams and passions.

For those whose passions are aligned with the business, further learning and training through the organization are possible by encouraging mentorship programs. Once in place, it's important to follow through at regular intervals to ensure that the mentor and mentee relationship is working.

Remaining Consistent

It's difficult for employees to get behind a leader who is constantly changing their vision, values, or point of view. Consistency is a vital ingredient for any worthwhile leader who wants to create employees that are prepared to follow them to the ends of the earth. Consistent leaders ensure that their communication is aligned with the vision and mission defined by the company, or the project specific to the team.

Work to Become A Leader People Like

Becoming a leader that people like means more than treating your position as a popularity contest. It's choosing to do things that are often unpopular and uncomfortable, but doing them anyway. Make sure that you're both open to change and new ideas as they come. We know that the business landscape continues to change and evolve almost daily. It's better to develop the attitude of "let's find a way of doing things better together," and then be prepared to change if you must. Be prepared to alter from a fixed mindset of "this is how we've always done it," to a growth mindset of "let's try and solve things using new ideas this time and see how it goes."

Great leaders handle problems as soon as they arise, rather than allowing them to fester and become bigger than they need to be. They understand that when you're working with different personalities, there will always be clashes and commotion no matter how effective they are at leading. Great leaders don't try and stifle these personal differences, instead, they act as facilitators and allow individuals to experience these scenarios for themselves. They don't take sides in these situations; instead, they are both fair and non-judgmental.

Excellent leaders aren't afraid of admitting that there's lots that they don't yet know. They constantly strive towards improvement by making use of every opportunity to learn and grow. They're not afraid of encouraging those they lead to do the same because they understand the value of knowledge. Employees respect these characteristics, and many will even try and model their own behavior on the attributes of a great leader. This opens the door to succession planning that's effective within organizations that have the track record for promoting from within.

Team Building

Team Assessment

Leaders cannot be effective in their day-to-day responsibilities without the support of a good team behind them. So, what defines a good team member? These are ideally individuals who can work both independently and as part of a team. They're driven to achieve the goals set out for them by their leader if it is communicated clearly. Teams should be regularly assessed to make certain that everyone within the team is in the very best position. Leaders should monitor everyone within their team without making them feel as though they're being smothered. If someone happens to be functioning better within another role, don't be afraid to move them into that role (even for a trial period); you never know when someone is going to discover their passion for something they didn't even know they had.

Team assessments can take the form of formal assessments, carried out bi-annually or quarterly. Other assessments can take place on the spot or spur of the moment when the team member least expects it. Assessments are an important way to get to know each member of your team better. It allows you to find out what their hopes and dreams are for the future, and you could even discuss ways to achieve their goals. Happy employees give of their best and remain loyal to the organization.

Motivate Your Team

There are several ways to keep your team motivated and moving in the right direction. One of the most important ways to do so is to lead from the front and lead by example. It's also about being able to act as a cheerleader whenever necessary and provide encouragement from the sidelines. This means still allowing your team to grow and thrive both as individuals and collectively. Ways to motivate your team in the workplace are only limited by your creativity. These could include team-building events, weekend getaways to brainstorm new ideas for a project, introducing different colored clothing for different teams within the organization, inviting guest speakers on a regular basis to boost team morale, or even watching applicable TEDx talks or YouTube videos.

Simple competitions to motivate towards project completion could help you reach tight deadlines. Regular awards or rewards could be offered as part of an incentive program like the international call center I mentioned earlier on. Whatever you decide to do, you will find your employees becoming a lot more engaged in the work process.

As a sidebar: It's not about the value or price tag attached to the reward that counts, as much as the team-based incentive. You are looking at creating an environment that is filled with positive and healthy competition. What's most important is that you, as the leader, follow through with whatever you promise.

Empower Your Team

One of the best ways to empower your team is by stepping back, releasing the reins, and allowing those on your team to take control of themselves. This will often be a great way to measure performance, supervisory skills, and many other attributes that team members might possess. If you're too close to the situation, it's easy to overlook these positive characteristics, or for them to get lost in the day-to-day functioning of the business.

An important part of empowering your team is allowing them to fail, knowing that you will still be there as a means of support. Those who have experienced failures or setbacks should be encouraged to continue in their efforts. It's important for leaders to reassure these individuals that failure is part of growing, and help them identify the lesson to be learned.

Provide Job-Specific Training

Great leaders ensure that their team members know exactly what's required of them and by when. If they're in need of any job-related training, it's part of your responsibility to ensure that this happens. It is also up to you to ensure that they have whatever tools are needed for them to be able to fulfill their work obligation to the organization. This could mean specialty software to be able to be effective, or other office equipment. Deadlines can depend on a multitude of things, from knowledge-based operations to technical support, due to faulty equipment. As the leader of any team, it should be your responsibility to ensure that the wheels are kept in motion, moving the work of the organization forward.

Lead Teams

Teams often need direction, and good leaders can lead in all directions. This means that they're effective in leading from the top downwards, from the bottom upwards, and able to lead effectively sideways. They can organize teams according to their specific strengths for optimum value of each individual team member. It's all about understanding how to maximize these strengths by planning work strategically, rather than flying by the seat of your pants.

Not all teams have strong individuals who are prepared to step out of the shadows and take the lead when necessary, and it's at times like these when leaders need to be specifically cognizant of this. When this happens, it may be worthwhile appointing someone to take control of the project and be responsible for reporting back on progress. That way, you are gently assisting them to take on new responsibilities, teaching them how to delegate and communicate; and while they may not realize it at the time, you're forcing them out of their comfort zone.

Encourage Loyalty

One of the largest challenges in business today is how to gain loyalty from your employees without forcing it upon them. Loyalty today is way different than in the past, when the silent generation or baby boomers were the majority in the workplace. The business model has completely changed with Generation-X, Millennials, GenY, and even some GenZ replacing these stalwarts of society. Each of these new generations has completely different ways of working, and according to the Gallup Business Journal, the statistics from a recent survey on Millennials tell the whole story:

- They are the generation that's most likely to change jobs

- 60% confirm that they are open to considering other opportunities

- Most millennials have totally zoned out of their current jobs

Therefore, coming up with solid retention strategies is vitally important for the modern leader. And, it's just as important to ignite a flame of passion within this generation to keep them active and engaged in the workplace. Without it, although they turn up for work, they already have one foot out of the door (Gallup Business Journal, n.d.).

Retention Strategies

High staff turnover is one of the largest challenges facing organizations and leaders over the last decade or so. As Millennials take over and become the single largest working group in the U.S. at present, controlling what HR professionals, hiring managers, and recruiters refer to as the "churn" of staff is their single biggest human resource challenge. Rehiring quality replacements often cost organizations double the previous incumbent's salary and then there is an expenditure that are seldom calculated:

- Retraining of a new hire

- Loss of proprietary information with ex-employee

- Client frustration waiting for replacement employees to learn your way of doing things

- Ability to work as a cohesive team once trusted has been re-established

It's much better to have a firm retention strategy in place, with ways to retain top talent within your organization, than having to replace them once they leave. This can include anything from competitive salaries to offering flexibility regarding where they operate. Remote work is becoming more in demand now than ever before, as Millennials make lifestyle choices rather than being chained to a desk in a small cubicle. They want the freedom to make their own decisions. Once you have their buy-in, they will be loyal to your organization and give you their very best work.

Vision

According to Kristi Hedges, executive coach, leadership development consultant, speaker, and author of *The Power of Presence* and *The Inspiration Code*, she confirms that becoming an effective and efficient leader takes time. It's not something that you suddenly decide to do by waking up in the morning. It takes time, effort, and practice. There are likely to be many times when you fail before your team, and those responsible for you will begin to accept and follow your vision for the future (Hedges, 2018).

Vision is where it all starts. We've often heard that organizations have their own mission statements and vision of where they would like to see the organization go. As a smaller division of a major multinational organization, it's vital that your divisional goals and vision align with the greater, overall vision and mission as the backbone to whatever you collectively decide is right for your division. The following are some key criteria when it comes to developing the right kind of vision within an organization—the vision that employees will follow:

Everyone Has a Role to Play

Ensure that everyone knows what the vision is, how it connects back to the overall vision of the company or organization, and what specific roles each member of the team needs to play. Inclusion is important to secure buy-in from those who are uncertain whether or not they should be following two sets of directions. One as outlined by the organization's senior executive committee, and the other that's closely aligned with where the division or department needs to be moving towards. Like a well-oiled machine, everyone within the division has a vital role to play towards the achievement of divisional goals.

Faces Toward the Future

There's no point in deciding on visions or goals that are not going to propel you towards future achievement. You aren't looking to stagnate, but rather, want to encourage the members of your team to strive to be better and do better every single day. If you can encourage them to be even a fraction better today than what they were yesterday, imagine the impetus this could have on moving your team towards the right trajectory.

Inspires Followers

While it's often said (and I paraphrase) that "great leaders are supposed to create other great leaders", I would reason that the world would be unable to function effectively if there were only great leaders. There need to be followers too. Great leaders have the capacity to inspire their followers to achieve whatever it is that they've set their sights on. This could be anything from meeting specific project deadlines to meeting sales budgets. These leaders can monitor the temperature of the team, even from a distance, and continue to motivate them. This motivation needs to occur daily—even on those days when you, as a leader, simply feel like giving in and allowing someone else to take over for a while. It's on days like these that you need to drag yourself out of bed, put your best face on (even if it is a façade for the day), and remain positive for those who are following you into the business fray daily.

Keep it Visible

Your mission statement (as agreed upon with all involved parties) needs to remain visible for everyone. This may necessitate some out-of-the box thinking. Whether this means making a large enough sign that everyone has to pass several times a day, or something smaller that contains the vision statement that can be at each desk within the department, find a way for your people to be able to internalize this mission and goals. It should be able to inspire them towards greater achievement daily. Having to stare at a mission statement daily, or reading it daily, will ensure that it becomes part of the very fiber of everyone in the team. It will help them internalize the ethos behind the mission that you're trying to achieve as a collective group of individuals.

Maps External Terrain

This is one of the most important roles when working with mission statements at the divisional or departmental level. The idea is that the major, overarching mission of the organization features in your departmental vision somehow. As the leader of these individuals, it's your responsibility to help your team connect the dots between the global organizational vision and the departmental vision.

A real-life example of this was when Mary Barra, the CEO and Chairman of General Motors was still heading up the Global HR Division. Her vision was to reduce the size of the corporate dress code manual which was over 20+ pages in length. So how did she do it? She addressed the various divisions and passed the responsibility onto them, holding each employee accountable. She reminded leaders that they were responsible for hundreds of staff members, and budgets that ran into hundreds of thousands of dollars, if not more. If they were able to be trusted with people and money, surely, she should be able to trust them with how to dress. The new dress code manual (section), reads: "dress appropriately".

Chapter 8: Leadership Dysfunctions

"Not finance. Not strategy. Not technology. It is teamwork that remains the ultimate competitive advantage, both because it is so powerful and so rare."

~ Patrick Lencioni

According to Ozgur Savas and his study entitled *Impact of Dysfunctional Leadership on Organizational Performance,* as published in the Global Journal of Management and Business Research: Administration and Management, he says that everyone is so focused on reporting and printing about the positive characteristics of leaders, that nobody ever discusses those that are toxic or dysfunctional. Unfortunately, despite how little is written about it, the reality is that dysfunctional leaders both exist and can seriously impact a team negatively (Savas, 2019).

Various negative leaders have been given some of the following titles and we will discuss each of these briefly, as well as identify other ways that dysfunction can creep into the workplace. First up, there are several dysfunctional names awarded to those leaders who create havoc in their wake.

Abusive Leadership

Abusive leadership can be any form of leadership, management, or supervision where the leader is perceived to be abusive in the workplace. This abuse could be anything from constant verbal-abuse or aggressive behavior. Abuse could also be tearing employees apart in public (we discussed rewarding in public and criticizing in private), and this type of leader would get a kick out of creating public humiliation for employees. Part of the problem with abusive leadership is whether it's happening, or whether it's a perception on the part of the employee.

Advantages of Abusive Leadership

There has been some empirical research done to determine whether there are actual advantages to abusive leadership. These have identified a couple of areas that may be construed as positive and advantageous to employees:

Should there be a large enough gap between the leader and the "abused" employee, it may just spur them on to furthering studies to place them in line for a promotion. The same study mentioned that should these employees be reprimanded for making a mistake, they would be less likely to repeat the same mistake again (Zhu & Zhang, 2019).

Authoritarian Leadership

Examples of authoritarian leadership would be any of the dictators as recorded in history, such as Julius Caesar in ancient Rome, Fidel Castro from Cuba, Adolf Hitler from Germany, Robert Mugabe from Zimbabwe, and many others. This is not to say that authoritarian leadership is strictly linked to politics, because it isn't. This type of leader is only concerned about themselves, and what's in it for them. Although they are still responsible for teams, they seldom take the time to consult with them when decisions need to be made. Instead, they follow their own set of rules and guidelines.

Disadvantages of Authoritarian Leadership

Constant criticism from this type of leader reduces the overall morale of the team.

The skills of the group are limited to the skills of the leader. If team members are more qualified or experienced than the leader, this won't have any positive influence because the leader will constantly block them with their "I know best," attitude.

There is no room for growth under this style of leadership, which can frustrate employees, often leading employees to seek opportunities elsewhere.

This leader points out mistakes the moment they happen, and feedback is mainly negative.

This leader stifles innovation and creativity within teams. This can also frustrate employees and lead to staff turnover.

Machiavellian Leadership

This type of leadership is named after Italian born bureaucrat, Niccolo Machiavellian, who happened to write a "leadership" book titled *The Prince* in 1513. The book was filled with ways to manipulate others to do your bidding, or to conform to your way of thinking. By 1970, this leadership style was labeled as being hostile, toxic, and manipulative. For most Machiavellian leaders, it's about being able to control those reporting to them through whatever means necessary, including fear tactics, wielding power, open retaliation, and embarrassment of those beneath them. Machiavellians can also display narcissistic tendencies and cannot deal with failure. They are hostile, arrogant, and demanding of attention as they crave success.

The main problem with this style of leadership is that it leads to toxicity within an organization and irrational decision-making. They have no moral compass whatsoever, but demand being respected by others (even when they're clearly undeserving of this honor). When things don't go as planned, these individuals are the ones that will be first in line throwing temper-tantrums, finger-pointing always outward. They don't accept responsibility for failure or error. It's always as a result of someone else and never themselves. These leaders have the potential to destroy entire organizations (Schaeffer, 2018).

Narcissistic Leadership

How can you tell if you're working for a narcissistic leader? And what can you do about it? Marriage counselor and life/career coach, Kathy Caprino confirms several ways to identify these destructive individuals. Kathy worked as an attorney for a few blue-chip organizations, hating every moment of it, until she discovered her actual passion was still helping people, but as a coach, instead of appearing in a courtroom. During her tenure with these large organizations, she tells of many experiences working for and alongside narcissists and how destructive they can be (Caprino, 2011).

Some of their characteristics are that:

- Narcissists have mastered the art of lying (even to the point where you're certain they believe their own lies).

- Their most dangerous characteristic is the inability to challenge them—ever! This is where their power kicks in, and before you even know what's hit you, you'll have a box with all the little goodies from your desk in a box, marching towards the EXIT sign.

- They are completely unfeeling and can neither sympathize nor empathize with their team.

- They are rule-breakers unless the rules are made by them, and even then, it would only be as the rules were in their favor.

- They can create high-energy environments in the workplace purely based on their high degree of enthusiasm.

- They like to be surrounded by people who adore them.

- While they come across all charming in daylight, beware of the sting in the scorpion's tail.

Unpredictable Leadership

The unpredictable leader lives up to their name, blowing hot one moment and cold the next. Being efficient and effective as a team member reporting to an unpredictable leader can be frustrating. The amount of time and energy that goes into trying to determine what they want next creates an environment where there is plenty of lagging, and little genuine progress in being able to move forward. If you are this type of leader, you need to come to terms with the fact that you're not "keeping your staff on their toes," by being unpredictable. You are setting the team up for frustration and failure. The main frustration comes as they're scrambling to predict your next move, instead of being able to synchronize with you.

The ideal working environment should have a leader that creates harmony and a cohesive unit, all working towards a common goal, rather than part of a dysfunctional team.

Management Skills

We have covered a lot of management skills that crossover as leadership skills as well. With honesty and integrity, for leaders it's important not just to be yelling and telling employees what to do. They need to hold themselves accountable to the same set of standards.

Decision-making in Leadership

Before diving into specific types of decision-making in leadership, what's most important of all is that decisions are made. It can be said that making a bad decision is better than no decision. Indecision in itself is already a decision that's been made. Successful leaders go from decision to decision as quickly as possible. Even if the decision that they've made doesn't pan out, they are able to change course and move in another direction with their team backing them up all the way.

Lean Management

Lean decision-making in a management context is a means to cut out delays in the decision-making process, which is experienced in virtually every organization globally. Managers and leaders are faced with multiple challenges, problems, or even conventional decisions that need to be made every single day. By implementing a Lean decision-making approach, organizations are able to make decisions a lot quicker than they normally would have. Decisions are also spread throughout the workforce, ending the finger-pointing blame game.

Lean decision-making happens when several staff members are empowered with decision-making for and on behalf of the organization, or as part of a specific project. Because the decision is made collectively, no single individual can be held responsible should the decision be the incorrect one. The team is empowered with the ability to course-correct should the decision be incorrect, and they're encouraged to base all decisions on as many facts, figures, and information that they can possibly acquire. With Lean decision-making, it's encouraged to leave decisions for as long as possible, while data and information are collected. This would result in the decision being based on as many facts and evidence to support the decision as possible.

Lean decision-making has been proven to be more transparent, predictable, and positive than when systems were not present (Simons et al., 2016).

Problem Solving

One of the biggest challenges when it comes to problem-solving in leadership is that you get some leaders who are extremely good at it. To the point where they can immediately pick up that there's a problem, they can trace the problem back to its root cause and they're able to resolve it in hardly any time at all. You may be asking why this type of skill could present a challenge for leaders? In truth, if a leader can analyze, diagnose, and repair rapidly on their own, what's the point of being surrounded by a team? Apart from this, how is any member of this leader's team meant to learn and grow on their own? Learning is acquired from physically doing, which means that for team members to grow into effective leaders themselves, they must begin somewhere. They need to learn and to grow through shared experiences. You, as their leader with exceptional problem-solving abilities, can make use of this exceptional teaching moment to share these skills with those who would like to learn how. Of course, the scale and scope of every single problem are likely to be different and unique. This is what makes it so exciting for your team members.

For some, it will take a deep-dive analysis of the problem. For others, it may need in-depth research into the mechanics of how something works.

One of your key responsibilities as a leader is to solve problems effectively. The strange thing about having to deal with problems is that they seem to be never-ending, and you no sooner deal with one and another one starts. According to a high-performance leadership coach, Glenn Llopis, it's not really the problem that's the problem; it's not having enough time to deal with the problem effectively from the start. He suggests the following four ways that leaders use to solve problems (Llopis, 2013).

Communication needs to be transparent with everyone involved on the various levels feeling as though they are free to engage in open dialogue as part of a team.

Following through with transparent communication comes the breaking down of divisional or individualized silos that people, departments, or organizations place themselves in. It's being able to identify where each staff member belongs, and enabling them with a free, safe space in which to operate.

The third step, according to Llopis, is for individuals to be open-minded so that the road to change and problem-solving can be as short and unencumbered as possible. Individuals who are open-minded aren't afraid to take risks and because of this, problems are solved much quicker than under normal circumstances.

The final step is strategic change. It's not good enough in problem-solving to substitute or stick a band-aid over it. Instead, genuine problem-solving requires radical change, improvement, and replacement. This replacement may be anything from policies and procedures to physical equipment to resolve recurring issues (Llopis, 2013).

Where problems are concerned in organizations, they will always be there, although no two problems are likely to ever be the same. Effective leaders can take charge in these situations, no matter how uncomfortable or unpleasant they may be. They are prepared to make some tough decisions and calls if that's what's necessary to fix what may be currently broken.

Process Improvement

Every organization and department run on a specific set of rules and guidelines, often referred to as policies and procedures. Even within a manufacturing environment, there are specific tasks or process flows that need to happen one after another. It would be impossible for an accountant to do the books for two months in advance when (s)he doesn't have any viable data to be working from.

Process improvement is being able to optimize specific organizational tasks, structures, policies, procedures, or processes to make the organization operate at its optimum capacity or level of efficiency. As a leader, it's your responsibility to ensure that your division is running at its best. Some of the ways to achieve this are to closely analyze the area you've either identified as having a problem, or the division you may want to optimize. One of the best ways I've discovered is by paying close attention to process flow just by quietly watching how things are handled. Is there somewhere that the business "flow" appears to hit a snag or a bottleneck? If so, how can this be rectified? For process improvement to be successful, you need complete transparency. If you know that your department is always on their best behavior when you're around, hire an external third-party that poses absolutely no threat to them whatsoever.

It's easy for those reporting to you to open to a neutral third party. Even running blind or anonymous questionnaires could prove valuable when you're either looking for a cause for inefficiency. As a strong leader, should change be necessary, it should be managed effectively in- house by yourself. This is where things can become uncomfortable, especially if tough decisions need to be made. What's most important, however, is that everything that happens should be in the best interest of both the organization and employees. The more win-win's you're able to notch up, the more your team will want to collaborate and work with you on making things better for all.

Crisis Handling and Conflict Resolution

Identify Good & Bad Conflicts

This is almost like addressing the elephant in the room in the workplace, yet it's one of the topics that most leaders shy away from. Unfortunately, whether you like it or not, crisis handling and conflict resolution are part of your role as a leader. It's your job to be dealing with it and rather than trying to avoid it, the best thing to do is to engage and minimize the fallout as quickly as possible.

Whether we'd care to admit it or not, we are all social beings, and each one of us is different. There are many individuals in the workplace who are out for blood and whose sole purpose or adrenaline rush for the day comes from the creation of sheer chaos, mayhem, and havoc. These individuals will do anything to manipulate those around them as best they can. As a leader, it's your job to recognize what is happening as quickly as possible, and to handle each of these situations with as much grace and ease as you possibly can.

Consider All Sides

Leaders should be unbiased and fair whenever it comes to conflict resolution. This means not picking sides from the get-go, and being prepared to consider all sides from every angle. While conflict resolution comes along with every job in every industry, it's best to not let it fester. Instead, seek amicable solutions that are fair to all parties concerned. I'm not advocating for one moment that an individual should prove to be more guilty of a serious offense that carries higher penalties and be treated less harshly. In fact, this is part of being a leader—making the tough calls whenever necessary. For example, if someone is guilty of corporate espionage, you're not going to hold the door open for them to leave with all your proprietary information. Instead, you are going to follow all the correct legal channels to ensure your organization is protected.

However, if they are being set up by someone else and this comes to light during your investigation, the act of slander and false accusations should also not be tolerated in the workplace. Remember that you're all spending most of your time at the workplace, so you should at least make it somewhere that people want to be. Very few people do drama very well in our fast-paced society. Make certain that employees and colleagues like and trust you. As they do so, you will be amazed at how much more you are able to get out of them than what they are currently doing.

Chapter 9: Leadership Communication

"Communication is a skill that you can learn. It's like riding a bicycle or typing. If you're willing to work at it, you can rapidly improve the quality of every part of your life."

~ Brian Tracy

Communicate Effectively

Without optimal, effective communication in leadership, no organization can thrive in modern society. As a leader especially, because you're responsible for so many diverse teams and individuals, communication could easily become a slippery slope. There's also a whole lot more to communication than sending out emails to those reporting to you or barking orders. According to the Center for Creative Leadership, "effective leadership and effective communication are intertwined."

Effective communication is being able to communicate successfully with a diverse group of people as individuals. No two people are the same, and it would be foolish to think that the way you communicate with one person would necessarily work in the same way when communicating with the next. Apart from this, there are subtle, yet distinct, differences between the way that you would communicate with your board of directors or a key client, and your team during a social event.

Have you ever considered that the way you communicate may be the reason why people either do what you want them to do or completely ignore your request, moving in the opposite direction? To become more effective in your communication with those around you, means understanding each of them individually, rather than collectively. When it comes to corporate communication and business leadership, this is one of the key areas that break-down (Center for Creative Leadership Blog, 2019).

Optimize Your Communication

Mastering the art of communication is a sure-fire way to improve your leadership skills and genuinely connect with your team. Leadership guru, John C. Maxwell, in his bestseller, *Everyone Communicates Few Connect: What the Most Effective People Do Differently*, redefines this "connection" in five categories, briefly summarized as (Maxwell, 2010):

Finding Common Ground

This is his first and most important rule in being able to connect with those around you, no matter the reason. Be aware that you need to see things from others' viewpoints, rather than your own. According to Maxwell, "It's difficult to find common ground with others when the only person you're focused on is yourself" (Maxwell, 2010).

Keeping Your Communication Simple

The world of communication is complex enough as it is at the moment, where almost everyone is trying to sound better educated and more knowledgeable than the next. While this may be necessary if you are writing for technical publications or academic papers, it's not necessary in the world of business. The best advice that I've ever received was from one of my editors when they indicated that every word should count, rather than writing towards the word count. Communication should be clear and straightforward so that your message cannot be misinterpreted. For this simple communication approach to work, Maxwell introduces a five-step strategy (Maxwell, 2010):

1.   Get to the point as quickly as possible.

2.   Repeat yourself three times so things are heard, recognized, and finally learned. This is how we each learn, through repetition and understanding.

3.   Communicate clearly and simply so that even a child can understand what you're trying to say.

4.   Saying less is often saying more, especially when you're trying to get a very specific message across.

5.   Talk to people and not above them. Even though you are the leader, you don't need to communicate with your team as though they are too dumb to understand.

Capturing People's Interest

This involves being able to be interesting to others, and what interests you is not always it. It's having those you're working with, speaking to, writing to, or addressing to be interested in what you have to say because it's done in such a way that it captures their interest and attention. Whatever medium you choose to use, the language and examples should reflect the target audience, and not always your own personal belief system.

Inspiring People Through Communication

Whether we realize it or not, we are communicating with those around us throughout the day. Some of this communication is verbal, while much of it is non-verbal. It's all the things that we don't actually say, but our face gets to say it, or body language gives it away. These skills form part of the self-awareness that we discussed earlier. They are also emotional intelligence attributes. You need to be self-aware of all the ways that you may be communicating your genuine emotions without meaning to.

Be specifically attentive to your body language. Open up, or make sure that during meetings you're not sending defensive signals to things people are saying. Watch out for folding your arms or crossing your legs, making your personal space smaller than it needs to be. Become the kind of communicator that people leave a meeting with the attitude, "that was really worthwhile, I got a lot out of it," rather than, "just another boring old meeting, nothing ever really happens. What a waste of time." (I'm sure that you've attended more than enough of these!)

Discovering the secret to inspiring those you lead really depends on the dynamics of your team. Some teams work well with morning meetings where they can air their opinions openly and discuss what needs to be achieved during the day. Others respond better to written communications in the form of individual, group, or team emails that are more specific and motivating at the same time. The main aim of this type of communication, whether verbal or non-verbal, face-to-face, or written, is that it achieves the objective of being able to motivate those in your team.

Staying Authentic in All Your Relationships

In his final tip, Maxwell indicates that the buy-in to a change in leadership within an organization and all the hype that goes along with it, usually only lasts for an average of six months. By that time, the leader would have had to have cemented their credibility that they are as genuine as they originally intended to be. They would have had to display that they are the type of leader they communicated they were. He refers to this as the "honeymoon being over" (Maxwell 2010). By this time, employees would have quickly identified whether the leader is authentic and trustworthy, that their word is their bond, or not.

Part of being authentic in relationships is not talking "down" to employees and then switching it up with your superiors. This is just fake, and your employees will pick this up really quickly. Don't try to be different from one group of people. Rather, stay true to your authentic self at all times.

Improve Your Communication Skills

Be an Active Listener. This is one of the most challenging areas for me personally, and I'm sure that I'm not alone. I really need to concentrate and be aligned with the individuals I am communicating with, and this involves physically being way more attentive to what they are saying verbally, as well as what they are saying non-verbally. What is their body language telling me? Am I listening with half an ear because I'm already trying to come up with the best solution to their concerns (when they haven't even finished voicing their concerns entirely yet)? Is it more important for me to hear my own voice rather than allowing the voices of my team to be heard, whether individually or collectively?

Be Professional, Rather Than a Comedian

This speaks to how well you know and interact with your audience. It's also important to understand that while you can be lighthearted some of the time during dialogue, passing on vital corporate information should not be done tongue-in-cheek, or in a way where the audience may consider the message to be a joke. It's more important to earn the respect of those with whom you're communicating than getting a laugh.

Beware of Body Language

Whether we care for the statistics or not, studies (Yaffe, 2011) have indicated that around 55 percent of how and what we communicate is nonverbal. This is done through a series of nonverbal cues and through our mannerisms. Most of the time, we aren't even aware that we have folded our arms, crossed our legs in a certain way, or chosen to make ourselves look like the shrinking violet in the room.

Communicate Key Points Effectively

Start and end your presentation by introducing what you plan to discuss in the meeting. Highlight each of these key points so they are clearly understood. By the end of your meeting, each of the key points discussed should be summarized to ensure the audience has understood what was discussed. This is an extremely effective method of communicating during meetings. The entire goal of this type of communication is to ensure that the audience is taking the right message away with them.

Encourage Audience Participation

The worst possible meetings are where one individual stands and does all the talking, while everyone else in the room becomes totally disengaged from what's happening. You can recognize that this is happening the moment individuals begin looking at their watches, the clock on the wall, checking their phones, doodling on paper they've brought with them etc. By asking important questions, you should be able to keep the attention of those in the room. You can be specific by addressing certain questions directly to one individual, asking for their take or feedback on the situation. Generally, the bored, glazed over look will only happen once if you take this advice. Others within the team will want to be prepared if they are called upon in the next meeting.

Make Sure Your Message Is Understood

Too often, we take for granted that people will understand exactly what we are trying to say, and will get the message right the first time, every time. This assumption is way off the mark. In order to understand things correctly, we need to repeat the same message several times. It's also worthwhile having the "audience" respond by letting you know what they perceived the message to be. This way, should there be any confusion, it can be clarified immediately.

Make Use of Technology Only When Necessary

While we have mentioned that PowerPoint should not be used as a medium for meetings, if you are likely to be giving the same presentation over and over again, it may be worthwhile to record it on platforms such as Zoom or Wistia. Each of these platforms allows the user to edit videos so they are at their best before being posted. These videos could be especially helpful when onboarding new employees.

Reduce Visual Aids

This relates to things like PowerPoint presentations. Avoid these at all costs. Both Steve Jobs, the late Apple CEO, and

Sheryl Sandberg from Facebook, eliminated the use of this medium within their organization as they discovered that they are not as helpful in getting the message across to individuals. Within each of these multi-billion-dollar industries, leaders have been encouraged to use their words, rather than relying on technology.

Request Feedback

One of the best ways to improve your communication skills is by asking for honest feedback from your colleagues, peers, and team members on a regular basis. We are often too close to a situation to recognize when there is a problem. Ensure that feedback is open and honest, even if you need to draw up a questionnaire that has relevant questions regarding the way you communicate that can be submitted anonymously.

Speak from The Heart

Another word for this type of communication is 'extemporaneous'. This is where you can write down several key points that you want to cover, yet you have not necessarily written out an entire scripted speech. This type of document allows you to communicate effectively by covering all the thoughts and ideas that you wanted to get across, while, at the same time, not being tethered to a formal speech where you read it verbatim. It allows you some creative latitude, and the speech doesn't come across as being rigid or forced.

Conclusion

"No man will make a great leader who wants to do it all himself, or to get all the credit for doing it."

~ Andrew Carnegie

Leadership in the 21st century is anything from straightforward and black and white. There are thousands of shades of grey that different organizations utilize to attempt to keep ahead of the pack or to inch out their competition. While the previous chapters have been as in-depth as possible, there is always much to be learned from other leadership experts, particularly those that are industry-specific.

Look to the past without becoming stuck there, for there are many lessons to be learned from many of the great leadership experts such as Napoleon Hill, Dale Carnegie, Jack Welch, and other giants of the old industry. Today, there are new leaders to mold and shape your career around. Look to each of these leaders for encouragement and guidance. Every conceivable industry has an iconic leader that is currently blazing a trail into the future. Find one that appeals to you, and study what they have done to make themselves who they are today.

Getting the basics right when it comes to leadership is the necessary first step. It's deciding the kind of leader that you'd like to be and then learning how to master each of the skills and characteristics of these leaders. In my humble opinion, servant-based leadership and situational-leadership suit my personal needs best. Remember that you can learn and develop those leadership characteristics you don't believe you currently possess. Although there are certain natural characteristics closely aligned with leadership that you could be born with, such as being able to convince others to follow you or having excellent communication skills, for most leaders, they need to discover many of these traits themselves.

In *Leadership 2.0*, you have each of these key characteristics and skills neatly laid out over each of the nine chapters where there are pearls of wisdom tucked away in each one. As promised, data substantiate each of the claims made, and statistics have been quoted. The information has been carefully researched and backed by empirical data to support each claim.

Strive to become an extraordinary leader by doing things differently. Identify the leadership style that works best for you and those around you. If you have a team that's mixed with a rich diversity of individuals, then situational leadership may be the best route to consider. Rather than settling for one style, you may need to switch it up depending on the conditions you're being faced with at the time. This may result in micro-managing certain individuals on your team during specific projects, whilst encouraging creative freedom from them at other times. This is how to master situational leadership. It requires flexibility and your willingness to change your style of leadership as often as required.

Remember that although certain leadership characteristics are potentially innate (meaning you're born with them), most of these skills can be learned and mastered over time. The key takeaway from this section is that you need to be consistent, no matter what. Individuals who battle to come to terms with the direction they should be heading in themselves cannot expect to be effectual leaders. Your path and direction should be so deeply ingrained in your mind that you ignite and display the passion of a great leader that individuals want to follow. Do the things that great leaders do by developing effective leadership habits. These begin with your daily habits. How you begin your day will set the tone for not only you, but for the rest of your team. Your mood when you're in the workplace will directly impact those around you. As a leader, it's best to leave any personal upheavals at the door. When your team sees you focused on what needs to be done, they will mirror your behavior.

The key to process improvement is constantly trying to reinvent yourself as a leader. A while back, there was a challenge on Facebook to maintain health and well-being during lockdown by doing push-ups. The goal was to start small, and add just a single additional push-up each day. This same process can be applied to leadership. You don't need to get it 100% right the first time. I know that I most certainly didn't. The goal is to see small, incremental improvements every day. Set yourself small, manageable goals that you know you can achieve. Like the single push-up, adjust the goal upwards slightly until eventually, you've mastered the area you wanted to improve.

With leadership comes the importance of managing yourself and who you are as a leader. This means being acutely aware of what you do and say. The most key takeaway when it comes to communication is that it's not always verbal. Our faces often say more than we'd like them to through micro-cues. These can be little things we're doing subconsciously. It's rolling our eyes at a comment we don't agree with, or raising an eyebrow, or moving your mouth in a certain direction. Add this to your arsenal of strategic ammunition regarding communication with others.

The single most important takeaway is that you need to discover your true authentic self as a leader and then work fiercely, passionately, and fearlessly to become the very best leader you have the potential to be. You now have the tools in your hands and at your disposal; what you choose to do with this information is completely up to you. You could use it to become the very best version of yourself you can be. Become the type of leader that others would want to follow, that they'd choose to look up to and emulate. Because leadership is constantly changing, you have the perfect opportunity to make yourself into whatever type of leader you'd like to be.

I hope that you will refer to this volume often, that each of the headings will inspire you, or provide you with relevant information that you need on your leadership journey in the 21st century. Remember that you have the potential for greatness, you just need to want it bad enough. Once you do, go after it with everything that you have, and a little bit extra for good measure.

Reach for your dreams in this brand new leadership landscape; it can be anything you want it to be!

Peter Allen

Premium Content

Subscribe to our receive premium content on productive meetings, business success, marketing mastery, sales conversion, team management and much more

Premium Content

Subscribe to our receive premium content on productive meetings, business success, marketing mastery, sales conversion, team management and much more

Name

Email

Send

https://www.subscribepage.com/premiumcontent

Access

References

Adkins, A. (2016, May 12). *Millennials: The job-hopping generation.* Gallup.Com; Gallup. https://www.gallup.com/workplace/231587/millennials-job-hopping-generation.aspx

admin. (2015, May 11). *My top 10 quotes on communication.* Virgin. https://www.virgin.com/richard-branson/my-top-10-quotes-communication

Andersen, E. (2012, December 16). Are leaders born or made? *Forbes.* https://www.forbes.com/sites/erikaandersen/2012/11/21/are-leaders-born-or-made/

Anthony, L. (2019). *Define situational leadership.* Chron.Com. https://smallbusiness.chron.com/define-situational-leadership-2976.html

Appian. (2017). *What is process improvement? | Appian.* Appian.Com. https://www.appian.com/bpm/process-improvement-organizational-development/

Bezos, J. (2020, July 28). *Statement by Jeff Bezos to the U.S. house committee on the judiciary.* US Day One Blog. https://blog.aboutamazon.com/policy/statement-by-jeff-bezos-to-the-u-s-house-committee-on-the-judiciary

Boiser, L. (2019, June 27). *End employee blame games with lean decision-making.* Kanban Zone. https://kanbanzone.com/2019/end-blame-games-lean-decision-making/

Bradberry, T., & Greaves, J. (2009). *Emotional intelligence 2.0.* Talentsmart.

Business News Daily Expert Editor. (2016). *5 Traits employees want in a boss.* Business News Daily. https://www.businessnewsdaily.com/9584-best-boss-traits.html

Caprino, K. (2011, December 12). *How to tell if your boss is a narcissist-- And 5 ways to avoid getting fired by one.* Forbes. https://www.forbes.com/sites/kathycaprino/2011/12/12/how-to-tell-if-your-boss-is-a-narcissist-and-5-ways-to-avoid-getting-fired-by-one/#5a1687ace08

Caprino, K. (2019, July 7). *Narcissistic leaders—the destructive lies they tell themselves and others.* Forbes. https://www.forbes.com/sites/kathycaprino/2019/06/07/narcissistic-leadersthe-destructive-lies-they-tell-themselves-and-others/

Center for Creative Leadership Articles. (n.d.-a). *Giving thanks will make you a better leader.* Center for Creative Leadership. https://www.ccl.org/articles/leading-effectively-articles/giving-thanks-will-make-you-a-better-leader/

Center for Creative Leadership Articles. (n.d.-b). *The importance of empathy in the workplace.* Center for Creative Leadership. https://www.ccl.org/articles/leading-effectively-articles/empathy-in-the-workplace-a-tool-for-effective-leadership/

Center for Creative Leadership Articles. (n.d.-c). *The irony of integrity.* Center for Creative Leadership. https://ccl.org/articles/white-papers/the-irony-of-integrity-a-study-of-the-character-strengths-of

Center for Creative Leadership Articles. (2017). *4 keys to strengthen your ability to influence others | CCL.* Center for Creative Leadership. https://www.ccl.org/articles/leading-effectively-articles/4-keys-strengthen-ability-influence-others/

Center for Creative Leadership Articles. (2018). *You can master the 3 ways to influence people*. Center for Creative Leadership. https://www.ccl.org/articles/leading-effectively-articles/three-ways-to-influence/

Center for Creative Leadership Blog. (2019, January 14). *What are the characteristics of a good leader?* Center for Creative Leadership. https://www.ccl.org/blog/characteristics-good-leader/

Cherry, K. (2014, June 25). *Situational theory of leadership*. Verywell Mind; Verywellmind. https://www.verywellmind.com/what-is-the-situational-theory-of-leadership-2795321

Cherry, K., & Morin, A. (2019). *How to become a stronger and more effective leader*. Verywell Mind. https://www.verywellmind.com/ways-to-become-a-better-leader-2795324

Cone, T. (2020, January 9). *What is innovation leadership?* Medium. https://medium.com/lightshed/what-is-innovation-leadership-8094f79620ca

Daskal, L. (2016, July 5). *Why the empathetic leader is the best leader - Lolly Daskal | leadership*. Lolly Daskal. https://www.lollydaskal.com/leadership/whats-empathy-got-leadership/

Downard, B. (2018, May 18). *101 Best leadership skills, traits & qualities - the complete list*. Brian Downard. https://briandownard.com/leadership-skills-list/

Doyle, L. (2019, March 7). *Leadership styles: 5 common approaches & how to find your own*. Northeastern University Graduate Programs. https://www.northeastern.edu/graduate/blog/leadership-styles/

Economy, P. (2015a, May 22). *7 Powerful habits for establishing credibility as a leader*. Inc.Com; Inc. https://www.inc.com/peter-economy/8-powerful-habits-to-establish-credibility-as-a-leader.html

Economy, P. (2015b, August 27). *27 Powerful quotes to bring out the real greatness in you*. Inc.Com. https://www.inc.com/peter-economy/27-powerful-quotes-to-bring-out-the-real-greatness-in-you.html

Ellevate. (2019, October 10). *Five combination traits of an effective leader*. Forbes. https://www.forbes.com/sites/ellevate/2019/10/10/five-combination-traits-of-an-effective-leader/#73fadf0654ad

Ewing, T. (2020, August 11). *7 Things mentally tough people never do—based on science*. Forbes. https://www.forbes.com/sites/tonyewing/2020/08/11/7-things-mentally-tough-people-never-do-based-on-science/

Forbes. (2020). *America's most innovative leaders*. Forbes. https://www.forbes.com/lists/innovative-leaders/#28c02f7b26aa

Furnham, A. (2010). The Machiavellian Leader. *The elephant in the boardroom*, 140–151. https://doi.org/10.1057/9780230281226_6

Future of Working The Leadership and Career Blog. (2018, September 4). *12 Advantages and disadvantages of dictatorial leadership styles*. FutureofWorking.Com. https://futureofworking.com/12-advantages-and-disadvantages-of-dictatorial-leadership-styles/

Gallup Inc. (2019). *How Millennials want to work and live*. Gallup.Com. https://www.gallup.com/workplace/238073/millennials-work-live.aspx

Garnett, L. (2015, August 26). *7 Steps to go from an ordinary to extraordinary leader.* Inc.Com. https://www.inc.com/laura-garnett/7-steps-to-go-from-ordinary-to-an-extraordinary-leader.html

Gifford, G. (2012, February 6). *Five keys to managing an unpredictable boss.* PrimeGenesis. https://www.primegenesis.com/our-blog/2012/02/five-keys-to-managing-an-unpredictable-boss-2/

Glassdoor Team. (2013, November 13). *Employers to retain half of their employees longer if bosses showed more appreciation; glassdoor survey.* US | Glassdoor for Employers. https://www.glassdoor.com/employers/blog/employers-to-retain-half-of-their-employees-longer-if-bosses-showed-more-appreciation-glassdoor-survey/

Half, R. (2018, November 7). *Effective employee retention strategies.* Roberthalf.Com. https://www.roberthalf.com/blog/management-tips/effective-employee-retention-strategies

Hasan, S. (2018, March 19). *Top 10 leadership qualities that make good leaders.* TaskQue. https://blog.taskque.com/characteristics-good-leaders/

Heathfield, S. M. (2004, October 9). *Leadership vision.* The Balance Careers; The Balance. https://www.thebalancecareers.com/leadership-vision-1918616

Hedges, K. (2018, October 25). *Don't have A leadership vision? Here's where to find it.* Forbes. https://www.forbes.com/sites/work-in-progress/2018/10/25/dont-have-a-leadership-vision-heres-where-to-find-it/#4787029da0a8

Inzlicht, M., Bartholow, B. D., & Hirsh, J. B. (2015). Emotional foundations of cognitive control. *Trends in Cognitive Sciences, 19*(3), 126–132. https://doi.org/10.1016/j.tics.2015.01.004

Jackowska, M., Brown, J., Ronaldson, A., & Steptoe, A. (2016). The impact of a brief gratitude intervention on subjective well-being, biology and sleep. *Journal of Health Psychology*, 21(10), 2207–2217. https://doi.org/10.1177/1359105315572455

Jacobson, S. (2019, July 26). *Teamwork: Respecting others.* The Conover Company. https://www.conovercompany.com/teamwork-respecting-others/

Kankousky, M. (2017, October 17). *7 strategies to boost your leadership skills through self-awareness.* Insperity. https://www.insperity.com/blog/self-awareness/

Kenny, H. (2017, February 27). *Are you an unpredictable leader? –Leading from the deep end.* Leading from the Deep End. https://leadingfromthedeepend.com/are-you-an-unpredictable-leader/

Koch, A. (2019, March 20). *5 Things employees really want in a boss.* Business.Com. https://www.business.com/articles/what-employees-want-from-leaders/

Kruse, K. (2018, May 18). 5 Things all employees want from their leaders. *Forbes.* https://www.forbes.com/sites/kevinkruse/2018/05/16/5-things-all-employees-want-from-their-leaders/

Kyocera Contributor, & Reaume, A. (2018, November 5). *Kyocera BrandVoice: What workplace decision-makers can learn from Lean manufacturing techniques.* Forbes. https://www.forbes.com/sites/kyocera/2018/11/05/what-workplace-decision-makers-can-learn-from-lean-manufacturing-techniques/

Lenkic, P. (2017, August 15). *Unpredictable leadership is dangerous, not disruptive.* SmartCompany. https://www.smartcompany.com.au/people-human-resources/leadership/unpredictable-leadership-dangerous-not-disruptive/

Llopis, G. (2013, November 27). *The 4 most effective ways leaders solve problems.* Forbes. https://www.forbes.com/sites/glennllopis/2013/11/04/the-4-most-effective-ways-leaders-solve-problems/

Lucas, S. (2020, May 1). *What do employees want most from their managers?* The Balance Careers. https://www.thebalancecareers.com/what-employees-most-want-from-their-bosses-4117080

Malsam, W. (2019, June 4). *Top down vs. bottom up management: What's the difference?* ProjectManager.Com. https://www.projectmanager.com/blog/top-down-vs-bottom-up-management

Maxwell, J. C. (2000). *The 21 irrefutable laws of leadership : follow them and people will follow you.* Struik Christian Books. (Original work published 1998)

Maxwell, J. C. (2010). *Everyone communicates few connect : what the most effective people do differently.* Jaico.

Myatt, M. (2015, December 13). *5 Keys of dealing with workplace conflict.* Forbes. https://www.forbes.com/sites/mikemyatt/2012/02/22/5-keys-to-dealing-with-workplace-conflict/

Oxford English Online. (2020). *Soft skills.* Oxford English Online.

Patel, D. (2017, March 23). 11 Powerful traits of successful leaders. *Forbes.* https://www.forbes.com/sites/deeppatel/2017/03/22/11-powerful-traits-of-successful-leaders/

Patel, D. (2019). *14 Proven ways to improve your communication skills.* Entrepreneur. https://www.entrepreneur.com/article/300466

Porter, J. (2014, October 6). *You're more biased than you think.* Fast Company. https://www.fastcompany.com/3036627/youre-more-biased-than-you-think

Porter, S. H. (2018, January 11). *Council post: You win or you learn: Risk-Taking for leaders.* Forbes. https://www.forbes.com/sites/forbescoachescouncil/2018/01/11/you-win-or-you-learn-risk-taking-for-leaders/

Qin, X., Huang, M., Johnson, R. E., Hu, Q., & Ju, D. (2018). *The short-lived benefits of abusive supervisory behavior for actors: An investigation of recovery and work engagement.* Academy of Management Journal, 61(5), 1951–1975. https://doi.org/10.5465/amj.2016.1325

Qualtrics. (2018, November 2). *10 Powerful quotes on leadership for your organization.* Qualtrics. https://www.qualtrics.com/blog/10-powerful-leadership-quotes/

Reynolds, J. (2018). *10 Leadership qualities to look for when hiring a manager.* Tinypulse.Com. https://www.tinypulse.com/blog/leadership-qualities-when-hiring-a-manager

Savas, O. (2019). *Impact of dysfunctional leadership on organizational performance.* Global Journal of Management and Business Research, 37–41. https://doi.org/10.34257/gjmbravol19is1pg37

Schaeffer, B. (2018, December 1). *Machiavellian leadership: how toxicity can lead to an organization's demise.* Www.Firehouse.Com. https://www.firehouse.com/leadership/article/210215131/ma

chiavellian-leadership-how-toxicity-can-lead-to-an-organizations-demise

Simons, P., Benders, J., Bergs, J., Marneffe, W., & Vandijck, D. (2016). *Has Lean improved organizational decision making?* International Journal of Health Care Quality Assurance, 29(5), 536–549. https://doi.org/10.1108/ijhcqa-09-2015-0118

Simplilearn. (2017, October 9). *Qualities of great leaders and great managers.* Simplilearn.Com; Simplilearn. https://www.simplilearn.com/leaders-and-managers-qualities-article

Singh, M. (2018, December 6). *Learning agility: How to measure it?* Mettl. https://blog.mettl.com/how-to-measure-individual-and-organizational-learning-agility/

Smarp Blog. (2020, August 6). *What are the top leadership skills that make a great leader?* Blog.Smarp.Com. https://blog.smarp.com/what-are-the-top-leadership-skills-that-make-a-great-leader

Smuin, A. (2017, July 13). *10 leadership skills every manager needs to succeed.* The CEO Magazine. https://theceomagazine.com/business/management-leadership/10-leadership-skills-every-manager-needs

SpriggHR. (2020a, January 8). *12 Essential leadership qualities • SpriggHR.* SpriggHR. https://www.sprigghr.com/blog/management-tips/12-essential-leadership-qualities/

SpriggHR. (2020b, January 13). *5 actionable employee retention strategies • SpriggHR.* SpriggHR. https://sprigghr.com/blog/management-tips/5-actionable-employee-retention-strategies/

Tech Support. (2013, October 17). *Problem solving ability.* The Complete Leader. https://thecompleteleader.org/problem-solving-ability

The Greenleaf Center for Servant Leadership. (2016). *What is servant leadership? - Greenleaf Center for Servant Leadership*. Greenleaf Center for Servant Leadership. https://www.greenleaf.org/what-is-servant-leadership/

Toffler, A. (1970). *Future shock*. Pan Books.

Tucker, R. B. (2017, February 10). *Six innovation leadership skills everybody needs to master*. Forbes. https://www.forbes.com/sites/robertbtucker/2017/02/09/six-innovation-leadership-skills-everybody-needs-to-master/

Walden University Blog. (n.d.). *What makes A good leader ten essential qualities to learn*. Www.Waldenu.Edu. https://www.waldenu.edu/programs/business/resource/what-makes-a-good-leader-ten-essential-qualities-to-learn

Wilbanks, C. H. (2018, August 22). *5 Ways to lead by serving*. The Wilbanks Consulting Group. https://www.wilbanksconsulting.com/blog/2018/8/22/5-ways-to-lead-by-serving

Wilson, A. G. (2015, March 26). *10 Most important leadership skills for team success*. ESkill. https://www.eskill.com/blog/important-leadership-skills-for-team-success/

Yaffe, P. (2011). *The 7% rule*. Ubiquity, 2011 (October), 1–5. https://doi.org/10.1145/2043155.2043156

Young Entrepreneur Council. (n.d.). *12 Employee Qualities That Managers Love*. The Muse. https://www.themuse.com/advice/12-ways-to-stand-out-to-your-boss-and-get-all-the-good-assignments-fun-projects-and-big-promotions

Zhu, J., & Zhang, B. (2019). *The double-edged sword effect of abusive supervision on subordinates' innovative behavior*. Frontiers in Psychology, 10. https://doi.org/10.3389/fpsyg.2019.00066

www.ingramcontent.com/pod-product-compliance
Lightning Source LLC
Chambersburg PA
CBHW071340210326
41597CB00015B/1518